SERMON
ON THE MOUNT

following Jesus in today's world

Martyn D. Atkins

For Helen – a Beatitude Person

ISBN 1 85852 223 4

© 2002 Martyn D. Atkins

Scripture quotations, unless otherwise stated, are from the New Revised Standard Version of the Bible, copyright 1989 by the Division of Christian Education of the National Council of Churches of Christ in the USA.

Printed by Newnorth, Bedford

SERMON ON THE MOUNT

SERMON ON THE MOUNT

following Jesus in today's world

JESUS' MANUAL OF DISCIPLESHIP

Sooner or later all those who consider themselves disciples of Jesus Christ have to come to terms with the Sermon on the Mount.

Like many classic texts, this Sermon is known of by lots of folk who have never truly read it. This short devotional guide is designed for groups and individuals wanting to study what many consider to be 'Jesus' manual of discipleship', and as such contains teaching which is at the heart of his message.

> *If I fail to understand this teaching, I fail to understand Jesus.*

As Philip Yancey puts it, 'If I fail to understand this teaching, I fail to understand him.' Suggestions for reflection and discussion are offered along the way, and readers are urged to 'go with the flow', taking time where time is needed and pressing on when they are ready. Consequently there are no defined 'sessions'. Groups should go at their own pace through this material and choose their own points at which to start and stop.

A HEALTH WARNING

A spiritual health warning must be given at the outset. The Sermon on the Mount has a habit of 'spiritually mugging' its readers! That is, you think you are studying the text only to discover it is studying you. This is quite normal, and is often a way God chooses to speak to us, to lead us on in our Christian discipleship. So expect the unexpected!

1

BE HONEST

As you study this Sermon, be honest with yourself, with others and with God, about your faith and life. Pretend piety is a tempting smokescreen but is deadly dull fellowship and rarely makes for spiritual growth. In fact, as you begin being studied by the Sermon on the Mount you might want to stop and consider honestly the state of your spiritual health. If you are in a group, share with each other 'where you are' in terms of your Christian discipleship as you begin this time of sharing and learning.

> *A Prayer as you begin:*
> *Lord Jesus, open your holy word to our lives and hearts, and our lives and hearts to your holy word. Amen.*

✳ ✳ ✳ ✳ ✳

MATTHEW'S MOUNTAINS

When Jesus saw the crowds, he went up the mountain . . .

(Matthew 5:1)

Matthew has a thing about mountains. For Luke it is journeys – go on a journey in Luke and God is going to meet with you or do something special.

> **How many 'journey stories' in Luke's writings can you think of where God shows up? Don't forget to include the book of Acts, Luke's 'volume 2' of the Christian story.**

But for Matthew it is mountains. Go near a mountain in Matthew and God is going to speak or act. It is Matthew who expands Mark's story of Jesus' transfiguration on a high mountain. He alone has Jesus' face 'shining like the sun',

Jesus is the new Moses and his teaching is the new Law.

just as Moses' face had shone after he had talked to God on another mountain (Matthew 17:1-8). This connection with Moses is important. God gave the Law – the *Torah* – from a mountain, and delivered it first through Moses. So here, when Jesus begins to preach on this mountain, the signal is unmistakable: Jesus is the new Moses and his teaching is the new Law.

THE BEATITUDES

(Matthew 5:3-11)

Then he began to speak, and taught them saying:

Blessed are the poor in spirit, for theirs is the kingdom of heaven.

Blessed are those who mourn, for they will be comforted.

Blessed are the meek, for they will inherit the earth.

Blessed are those who hunger and thirst for righteousness, for they will be filled.

Blessed are the merciful, for they will receive mercy.

Blessed are the pure in heart, for they will see God.

Blessed are the peacemakers, for they will be called children of God.

Blessed are those who are persecuted for righteousness' sake, for theirs is the kingdom of heaven.

Blessed are you when people revile you and persecute you and utter all kinds of evil against you falsely on my account. Rejoice and be glad, for your reward is great in heaven, for in the same way they persecuted the prophets who were before you.

I was travelling somewhere recently and got hopelessly lost. For once, it wasn't my fault. The person who had sent me the directions had got everything right except one thing – on the very first line of the instructions he told me to turn right on leaving the motorway, and he meant turn left! Only one word wrong. But the following 16 directions made no sense whatsoever!

I have a feeling that the same thing applies as we turn to the Beatitudes – these 'Blessed are . . .' statements with which Jesus begins his Sermon – a feeling of 'Get this wrong and nothing else will make sense.'

PEOPLE, NOT PROGRAMMES

Notice that Jesus begins his Sermon not with programmes or strategies, but with the character of *people*. In fact the whole Sermon is personal rather than programmatic.

Isn't 'with people' where God always seems to begin? The story unfolding through the Old Testament is full of great events and happenings, but they all relate to God's calling to people.

Supremely, God coming in Christ – the Incarnation – demonstrates God's deep commitment to people. Ultimately, when something needs doing for humankind that we cannot do for ourselves, God does not shout by megaphone from heaven, or send extraterrestrials, but sends himself in Jesus Christ.

Consequently when Jesus begins to talk about the 'kingdom of heaven', he doesn't outline the dimensions of the palace in Jerusalem, the rate of taxation to be levied, or the rules of the reign, but with the inner qualities and desires – the character – of kingdom people.

So we approach the Beatitudes in terms of *people* rather than doctrines, asking what kind of characters are Beatitude People?

WHAT KIND OF CHARACTERS ARE BEATITUDE PEOPLE?

Beatitude People are the kind of people God has on his wall!

If you were to walk round my house you would see various pictures and posters on the walls. One bedroom has wall-to-wall pictures of Leeds United players, because my youngest son is football crazy. Another is replete with rock groups, because another son is music mad. Our hallway is full of family photographs, constant reminders of loved and treasured ones each time you walk in the door.

Jesus suggests that if God put pictures on the walls they would be pictures of Beatitude People!

What sort of people come to mind when you read the Beatitudes? Share in the group those you have thought of, and why you thought of them as Beatitude People.

We look at some reasons why.

Beatitude People wear 'God's glasses'

What I mean is that Beatitude People seem to view the world like God does.

Jesus didn't invent Beatitudes. 'Blessed are'/'happy are'/'lucky are' statements are quite common in the Old Testament and inter-testamental literature and are technically known as macarisms. But these Beatitudes usually followed a pattern, and you'll recognise the groove: 'Blessed are the beautiful ones', 'Happy are the healthy ones', 'Lucky are the lucrative ones' etc., etc. That's the way it is! Isn't it?

Anyone who gets up and says, 'I'm going to tell you how to be truly happy and blessed' will get a crowd. So when Jesus begins 'Blessed are . . .' many folk on the mountain would think they knew what was coming. So they listen. And what does come? Words which whether spoken then or now stand everything on its head.

In a world where wealth equals success Jesus says, 'Blessed are the poor.'

In a world where pride and assertiveness are prized Jesus says, 'Blessed are the meek.'

In a world where not getting caught is the main aim Jesus says, 'Blessed are those who ache after what is right.'

In a world where ruthlessness is a desirable quality Jesus says, 'Blessed are the merciful.'

In a world where ripping people off, lying, promiscuity, betrayal, are 'just the way it is' Jesus says, 'Blessed are the pure hearted.'

In a world where 'living in the real world' means violence, hostility and killing Jesus says, 'Blessed are the peacemakers.'

In a world where keeping quiet, and not putting your head over any parapet is 'smart' Jesus says, 'Blessed are the persecuted ones.'

And in a world where respect and honour are much sought-after Jesus says, 'Blessed are those who rejoice when they are spat at, and reviled, and ridiculed, and persecuted.'

> When you read the Beatitudes did they sound like good news to you? Did you accept that the poor, meek, merciful were 'blessed' and 'happy'?

What kind of teaching is this? It is teaching which judges us, and like all judgement it reveals what we are. It reveals us to be non-Beatitude People.

Think! If you have read these words of Jesus and it hasn't sounded like good news then you have just judged yourself.

Beatitude people aren't likely to get elected!

A manifesto of poverty of spirit, mourning, meekness, thirsting after righteousness, mercy, purity of heart and peacemaking is not likely to catch many votes. You see, the gospel stands all human values on their head. The gospel is 'subversive' because it judges all human systems.

Imagine a sermon that begins: 'Blessed are you poor. Blessed are those of you who are hungry. Blessed are those of you who are unemployed. Blessed are those going through marital separation. Blessed are those who are terminally ill.'

The congregation does a double take. What is this? In the kingdom of the world, if you are unemployed, people treat you as if you have some sort of social disease. In the world's kingdom, terminally ill people become an embarrassment to our health-care system, people to be put away, out of sight. How can they be blessed?

The preacher responds. 'I'm sorry. I should have been more clear. I am not talking about the way of the world's kingdom. I am talking about God's kingdom. In God's kingdom, the poor are royalty, the sick are blessed. I was trying to get you to see something other than that to which you have become accustomed.'

S. Hauerwas and W. Willimon

What is the relationship between 'the kingdom of heaven' and 'this world'? How do you respond to Jesus' teaching that, ultimately, God's kingdom is full of Beatitude People?

In *The Clowns of God*, a novel by Morris West, Christ returns just as the world is about to blow itself to pieces. He returns particularly to whom? To the Clowns of God, that is, to the maimed, the handicapped, the rejected – his cherished ones.

Beatitude People have grasped a great insight. They know that the Beatitudes are not about what *we* think works, but about how *God* works.

The starting place of the Christian disciple is not one who says, 'Yes, Lord, I understand' or 'Yes, Lord, I am that kind of person' but 'Yes, Lord, you are that kind of God.'

> *The Beatitudes are not about what we think works, but about how God works.*

It's like those 3D pictures, where you squint, and concentrate then relax, and move the book up to your nose and away again – and what on the surface looks like an elephant is revealed to be something quite different. The kingdom of heaven, says Jesus, works quite differently to the kingdom of this world. God looks at things through a different set of lenses. Beatitude People wear God's glasses with which to look at the world. Are you wearing them?

Beatitude People adopt the right posture

'Blessed are the poor in spirit,
for theirs is the kingdom of heaven'

It would be best to have God's glasses on as we look at this, the first Beatitude.

I was in East Malaysia when I attended a session of a conference for women belonging to some of the indigenous tribes of Borneo and Sarawak. It was humbling to watch them as they kissed each other goodbye, their possessions, taped up in black bin liners, being thrown into the back of old, open-top lorries in which they would travel back to their remote villages. And I thought of my decent suitcases and what was in them . . .

Why are the 'poor' blessed? Monika Hellwig suggests some reasons why.

1. The poor know they are in urgent need of redemption.
2. The poor know not only their dependence on God and on powerful people but also their interdependence with one another.
3. The poor rest their security not on things but on people.
4. The poor have no exaggerated sense of their own importance, and no exaggerated need of privacy.
5. The poor expect little from competition and much from co-operation.
6. The poor can distinguish between necessities and luxuries.
7. The poor can wait, because they have acquired a kind of dogged patience born of acknowledged dependence.
8. The fears of the poor are more realistic and less exaggerated, because they already know that one can survive great suffering and want.

9. When the poor have the gospel preached to them, it sounds like good news and not like a threat or a scolding.

10. The poor can respond to the call of the gospel with a certain abandonment and uncomplicated totality because they have so little to lose and are ready for anything.

(listed in Philip Yancey's book *The Jesus I never knew*)

> **Try replacing 'The poor' with 'I'.**
> **eg. 'I know I am in urgent need of**
> **need redemption' etc.**

Now, with God's glasses on, do you see why they are blessed?

Jesus is not suggesting that the poor are blessed because they are poor. How could he? He spent his life, and urged his followers to spend theirs, striving to remedy such situations. Nor is Jesus suggesting that poor people are more holy or better than rich people simply on the basis that they are poor.

The poor have, quite literally, less to remove before they are naked before God.

Jesus is pointing out that it is the poor, with so little choice and with their acute need of dependency, who have an innate advantage over the comfortable and self-sufficient in relation to the kingdom of heaven.

Why are the poor blessed?

They are blessed because they are far more likely to adopt the right *spiritual posture* before God. It is possible to come before God brash, arrogant, but that's the wrong posture. Beatitude People adopt the right posture before God.

What is the posture of a Beatitude Person?

We know the posture of a boxer and a ballet dancer. What is the posture of a Beatitude Person?

Kneeling, humble, arms lifted in adoration, hearts and hands open and ready to receive from God.

We can link this to the second Beatitude:

'Blessed are those who mourn,
for they shall be comforted.'

Some biblical commentators suggest this means mourning over sin, that a person is blessed when a deep awareness of their inherent selfishness and impurity overwhelms them. Like the poor, such folk are more likely to adopt the right posture.

For many of us it is only when we realise our own helplessness that we permit God to do something with us. We enter the kingdom of heaven by being born again, and that takes humility. Dependence, sorrow, repentance, a longing to change – these are the gates to God's kingdom. It is very difficult for proud people to acknowledge their spiritual bankruptcy, but such is necessary if we are to be Beatitude People.

> **What is your spiritual posture before God? Is it the right one?**

The words of invitation to share Holy Communion in the Service for Lent and Passiontide in *The Methodist Worship Book* strike the right mood.

> *Come to this sacred table,*
> *not because you must but because you may;*
> *come, not to declare that you are righteous,*
> *but that you desire to be true disciples of our Lord*
> *Jesus Christ:*
> *come, not because you are strong,*
> *but because you are weak;*
> *not because you have any claim on heaven's*
> *rewards,*
> *but because in your frailty and sin*
> *you stand in constant need of heaven's mercy and*
> *help.*

Ultimately the Beatitudes pose questions about our character, our very selves.

Is 'what we are' based on our job, wealth, education, good looks, ability or arrogance? Or is 'what we are' based on our helplessness, our nakedness before God, on the hard business of throwing ourselves entirely on God's mercy and knowing, even as we do that, that God will not let us down?

Beatitude People put pie-in-the-sky-when-you-die on the menu!

All but the first and last Beatitudes are in the future tense. They describe those who *shall* be comforted, or satisfied, who *will* inherit the earth. Something good is coming in the future, but not now.

We need to note that there is a general rejection of this kind of thinking today. Pie-in-the-sky-when-you-die is not popular, and the very phrase is usually said with a sniff or a sneer. In the clamour for our 'rights', for self-gratification, now, this instant, pie-in-the-sky-when-you-die talk aggravates rather than appeals. Nowadays we want to take the waiting out of wanting. A hundred and fifty years ago folk missed a stagecoach and waited patiently till next week for another. Nowadays we miss the space on the revolving door into our local supermarket and spend the rest of the day playing 'catch up'! We used to be a saving card society, now we are a credit card society, and the difference is stark. Pie-in-the-sky-when-you-die is not flavour of the month.

It is easy to see why. With your pie-in-the-sky-when-you-die hat on, you might read the Beatitudes as simply 'sops' that Jesus offered to various sad cases of life. You might think Jesus is saying, 'There, there, here's a few words to make you poor souls feel a bit better.'

> *Pie-in-the-sky-when-you-die is only an empty promise when there is no pie!*

Such a view of what Jesus was about would be mistaken. You see, pie-in-the-sky-when-you-die is only an empty promise when there is no pie! If pie there is, then it's a whole different diet. So I want to defend pie-in-the-sky a little. Remember who Jesus is. He is the eternal Son of the Father. He knows a thing or two about heaven; 'my Father's house' he calls it. When Jesus – the Lord of heaven and earth – talks about it, it is not empty wishful thinking, it is heaven talk, and there's a world – even an eternity – of difference between the two. So when the Lord Jesus Christ says that those who mourn will be comforted, then they will!

At a meeting of the World Methodist Institute for Evangelism in January 2001 many stories were told. Some of them made me cry. Stories about our Christian sisters and brothers, many in appalling, seemingly unchangeable circumstances, whom you expected would have been crushed and broken – but were not. Instead, from Africa and South America alike they led the way in prayer and praise and worship and witness and authentic testimony. The hope of heaven burned in their hearts!

Are you going to tell these folk that pie-in-the-sky-when-you-die is nonsense?

Or have you ever visited a Christian near the point of death? Have you heard them talk about 'going home' as their body wastes away?

Are you going to tell them that heaven talk is pointless?

The contemporary fetish with 'now' – having it all in an instant – must be resisted. We are kingdom people, and God's kingdom is now and not yet. Therefore we are now and not yet people. We are God's people now, and we are preparing for eternity. That is the hope that holds Beatitude People together, and hope for future rewards is a good thing, because it is a gift from God.

Beatitude People know that the Beatitudes are genuine promises of Jesus, which are central to his message.

> **All this talk about future benefits and blessings – a faith hope or a futile hype?**

Beatitude People know that what God wants is good for them

Beatitude People really are blessed.

I know when I meet a Beatitude Person. There is something about them. Although they are almost always graciousness itself, they possess a richness of spirit that shines into my own poverty of spirit, and when I recognise that, I know this deep truth – Beatitude People really are blessed. It is not just pie-in-the-sky, it is that Beatitude People know that Beatitude living brings blessing in *this* life, here and now.

The word Matthew's text uses for 'blessed' is *makarios*, which, as near as we can do it (and apparently you can't do it at all in Welsh!), means, 'to be happy'. But that doesn't mean 'happy', in that 'Aah, vanilla milkshakes are back on stream at McDonald's' sense! It is, as James Jones comments, a word with a meaning far too substantial to be kept in a flimsy form like 'happy'. It means a deep sense of well-being, a sense of contentment that is real, a happiness that doesn't depend on what happens.

Keep God's glasses on and look at some more of the Beatitudes, and see if this truth becomes clearer.

'Blessed are the meek, for they will inherit the earth'

I like chat shows. I suppose I am naturally nosy about other people's lives. On they come, smiling, shining, happy people. The stars of music, screen and sport. Yet under all the hype and glamour the stars are, it appears, a pretty miserable lot. Their affairs, excesses, therapies, problems and remedies make copy for umpteen glossy magazines and newspapers.

Alongside these 'stars' are those we might call the 'servants'. The relief worker in India, the lawyer who gave up a lucrative career to run a free advice service for Palestinians in

Bethlehem, the medical doctor who left a suburban surgery and moved into an inner city clinic. Low pay, no pay, long hours, brings its own stresses and strains. But you talk to them, and you know, deep inside, that there is a richness and a joy. It just oozes out of them. In the process of losing their lives, they find their Real Life.

> Meekness is essentially a true view of oneself, expressing itself in attitude and conduct with respect to others . . . the one who is truly meek is the one who is truly amazed that God and man can think of him as well as they do and treat him as well as they do.
>
> Martyn Lloyd Jones

You see, in the kingdom of God, the way up is down. These 'servants' are Beatitude People. They *are* the blessed ones. Theirs is the kingdom of heaven, and they will inherit the earth.

'Blessed are the merciful, for they shall be shown mercy'

The story of Henri Nouwen is well known. He was a leading academic who gave up his academic career several years ago in order to care full-time for Adam, a seriously disabled man. Philip Yancey recalls interviewing him, 'Couldn't someone else look after Adam? Wouldn't you be better writing and lecturing?' It suddenly dawned on Yancey that Nouwen was genuinely coming at the thing from completely the other way round. 'What have I given up?' said Nouwen. 'It is I, not Adam, who gets the main benefit from our friendship', and as if he couldn't believe that the question had been posed, Nouwen returned to the advantages and benefits of caring for Adam several times in the conversation. He is blessed, and when it really counts, he will be shown mercy.

'Blessed are the pure in heart, they shall see God'

In terms of straightforward Christian doctrine, this makes perfect sense. One of the results of impurity – sin, if you like – is separation from God. The sinful are separated from God. The removing of sin and the coming of righteousness restores us to God.

In this sense we are all responsible to some extent for the limits of our relationship with God. Whenever I harbour lust, hate or any other impurity, the knock-on effect is that I limit my own intimacy with God. Put simply, there is simply not enough room for both sin and God to exist within us.

That is why it is the pure in heart who will see God, because space has been created and barriers

What are the things in your life that you suspect prevent you from 'seeing God'?

are removed. And after all, how can it be that you see God and are not blessed?

'Blessed are those who hunger and thirst after righteousness'

This is perhaps the catch-all attitude of the Christian character. At the heart of these Beatitudes is a passion for righteousness.

At a conference in Amsterdam in 2000 it was discovered that an African Christian had sold his corn intended for the next year's harvest in order to attend the conference. Some said he was a fool. He said it was worth it in order to be better equipped to share the gospel of Jesus Christ.

What about us? Do we approach the Lord's table like famished souls or someone complaining that it's just bread and wine again?

What we hunger and thirst after signals what really matters to us.

Are we those who hunger and thirst after *righteousness*? Beatitude People do, and they are blessed.

Beatitude People know that happiness is a by-product

Have you noticed a common factor in all these Beatitude characters? For each of them, being blessed/happy is a by-product and not the goal itself. Isn't that ironic? We seek and strive and try for our own happiness and still finish up opening the fridge door late at night, looking at all the food and saying, 'I don't know what I want'! It seems that God has so constructed the world that the search for our own happiness will always be self-defeating, precisely because it is the search for our own happiness. God has designed the world differently to that. Those who search for the deep qualities that enrich life and enrich others are the ones who find true happiness – as a by-product.

So, however tempting and culturally acceptable it may be, as followers of Christ we must beware of the search for self-fulfilment. The Beatitudes suggest that if the world is to be put right it will happen only and when I deny myself some self-fulfilment that others might have some. Instead of getting hung up about self-fulfilment, let's get hung up on the Beatitudes and let self-fulfilment take care of itself.

Those who invest in others, take courage in the face of injustice, are with the weak and needy, pursue God and not self, *they are blessed*. They get filled while others remain empty. Here is the clue to life in all its fullness. Do what Jesus did and give it away in pursuit of God and God's kingdom. If you want to, truly want to, you'll find that you can.

> **Am I hung up on self-fulfilment?**
> **What would it mean for me to get**
> **'hung up' on the Beatitudes?**

SALT AND LIGHT

(Matthew 5:13-16)

You are the salt of the earth; but if salt has lost its taste, how can its saltiness be restored? It is no longer good for anything, but is thrown out and trampled under foot.

You are the light of the world. A city built on a hill cannot be hid. No one after lighting a lamp puts it under a bushel basket, but on the lampstand, and it gives light to all in the house. In the same way, let your light shine before others, so that they may see your good works and give glory to your Father in heaven.

Beatitude People are the Salt of the earth

Any seasoned sermon listener has been peppered with information about the role of salt in the ancient world. Nevertheless, if Jesus calls this group of folk 'salt people', we do well to remind ourselves what he might be getting at.

> **How many uses of salt can you think of? Make a quick list.**

You will probably have noted that salt was – and is – used as a preservative. That is, it prevents things from

> **How do we best proclaim the gospel message of God's salvation today?**

perishing. Is Jesus talking about the kind of people who embody the message that God wants to save everyone from perishing?

In what ways do you think Christians should be 'distinctive' today?

You will probably also have noted that salt is associated with seasoning, that it brings out flavour, that it is very distinctive. In the ancient world, salt was used in healing.

Did you notice that in each example salt is used in relation to *something else*? It is always added, or introduced, or administered. In fact, unused salt is pretty much useless. At the end of the street where I live is a yellow plastic bin, full of rock salt. But the street stays icy if the salt stays in the bin. Salt in a sachet is still salt, but what good is that? It is only of use if it is used. It is when salt comes together with something else that we see its impact.

It seems clear, therefore, that when Jesus talks about his hearers being 'salt of the earth' he is talking about people who are committed to engagement, not escapism, on earth. That is why Rebecca Manley Pippert called her book on evangelism *Out of the Saltshaker*, because salt people who don't mix with anyone are just useless.

For many Christians this challenges our perception of what it means to be holy. We often associate holiness as 'apartness' and 'separation' and this has sometimes led to the Christian Church becoming something of a religious ghetto. Sadly we are often characterised by what we do *not* do, rather than what we do!

Jesus gives nine characteristics of a Beatitude person – a 'blessed' character of real holiness – and each image, like salt, implies engagement, not disengagement.

What would it mean for our local church to take seriously this call to engagement with the world? To what extent would we have to change our invitations to 'come and join us' into models of mission where we 'go' in Christ's name?

There is not one suggestion in this Sermon that being a Beatitude Person is achieved or attained by opting out, or hiding away from the world in which we live. In Christian discipleship then, there are no grounds for opting out of the world. Worldliness must be resisted, most certainly, but this does not mean opting out of the world, a world Jesus died to save. The world, with all its muck and squalor and compromise, is the environment in which Jesus clearly calls his followers to be salt.

There is also a severe word of warning here. What happens if the salt becomes saltless? It can happen. It does happen. Salt, in Jesus' time, often meant potash, fertiliser. In the ancient world rock salt could become useless – then it was called dirt! Salt that has lost its saltiness is effectively non-salt. If Christian disciples fail to be 'salt people' are they disciples at all?

> *We don't know how to be the church, because we don't quite know how we are supposed to live in the world.*
>
> Mike Regele

If Jesus' disciples are doing the 'salt people' bit properly, one other thing is true. People become thirsty. Thirsty for the same God and the same gospel that gives Christian disciples their distinctive 'flavour' and crucial role in God's world.

Beatitude People are the Light of the world

Those knowledgeable about the gospels will immediately note a problem here. Jesus said *he* was 'the Light of the world'. So how can his followers be? One clear answer presents itself – what Jesus is, his disciples are to be.

Does what people <u>see</u> and what they <u>hear</u> from Christians match up? Do our lives and lips agree?

But there is a difference. We, as Christian disciples, are not the *origin* of the light, its source is not down to us and we don't produce it. Take a light bulb out of its power supply, and though there may be nothing wrong with it, it will not shine. We derive any light we have from Jesus Christ, the Light of the world, and he is the one to whom we bear witness. As Charles Price reminds us, our making the light a thing of boasting or self-importance is like a light bulb congratulating itself on shining!

I visited a church recently where some renovation had been done. As we went from newly decorated room to room the steward flicked the light switches and gloomy lights came on. When I commented on the gloom she explained that they had fitted the whole church with 40 watt bulbs in order to save electricity! It seems to me that many Christians and churches opt to run on a lower output than the Light of the world would supply.

Taken together, Salt and Light give two complementary pictures of Christian witness and mission. Salt affects what it touches, light affects a much broader area.

One time while I was on holiday in France there was a tremendous electrical storm. I watched it cross the sky in the middle of the night. But it was the lightning that first woke me, not the thunder, and in terms of Christian witness it is often what you *see* rather than what you hear which is the crucial factor.

I consider that what the world needs, what our society needs, is not better or more salespeople of the gospel but more 'free samples'. People today

> *What the world needs is not better or more salespeople of the gospel, but more 'free samples'.*

don't just need telling that the gospel is good news, they need to experience good news people. Get that right and many of our concerns about decline and the state of the Church will take care of themselves.

> *Beauty of life causes strangers to join the ranks . . . We do not talk about great things; we live them.*
> A Christian writer about AD150

In describing his followers as Salt and Light, Jesus leaves us in no doubt that Beatitude People are missionary, evangelistic people. Beatitude People are holy people because they are Salt and Light.

Beatitude People are total characters

A schoolteacher who had spent all week invigilating public examinations was asked to read the scripture lesson in church on Sunday morning. The lesson set was the Ten Commandments. She read it beautifully then, in a great example of 'automatic pilot' concluded, 'Only four of these need to be attempted in the allotted time'!

When Jesus set out these Beatitudes he was not inviting his hearers to choose a couple and leave the rest. Christian discipleship is not a buffet! The whole person is being described. Instead of talking about 'whole life' discipleship, perhaps we should be asking if there is such a thing as 'part-life' discipleship?

Each of us, by our natures, will be able to manage some of the Beatitudes better than others, and we try to get along on those Beatitudes, to

> How are we doing in relation to Beatitude characteristics, which we don't feel 'come naturally'?

play to our strengths. The test of righteousness, however, is how well we are doing in respect of those things to which we are *not* naturally inclined. How's that going?

> Have you noticed how the fruits of the Holy Spirit Paul lists in Galatians 5 run so closely to the character profile produced by this list of Beatitudes? Is that a clue as to whose power is indispensable to the formation of such a character?

Beatitude People know there is a price to be paid
'Blessed are the peacemakers'

In Hebron, right on the flashpoint line between Israelis and Palestinians, is the Christian Peacemaker Team (CPT). This group of mainly US and Canadian Mennonites and Quakers are committed to prayer and action for peace. Each day they introduce themselves to whoever is in charge of the Jewish soldiers and urge that there be no trouble. Then they go into the Arab community, where they are known, and counsel peace.

One of their special jobs is to escort Arab children to a local primary school. The children's mothers used to do it, but it is right next to a wire fence and some Jewish women used to stand in wait and throw stones and spit at the Arab women and their children as they walked just a few feet away on their way to school. Now the CPT acts as a human barrier and takes the spit and stones.

Or if a house is to be bulldozed (as many are) they go and sit in it. Or if trouble breaks out, they run into the middle of it, in pairs, one going to the Israeli soldiers urging them to put down their guns, the other to the Palestinian youths urging them to put down their stones.

Jesus said, 'Blessed are the peacemakers and those who are persecuted for righteousness' sake.'

There is a price to be paid for this kind of character. People insult you, persecute you, swear falsely against you, often on account of your faith in Christ. Jesus says, 'Rejoice and be glad!'

In what ways might we confuse charity with justice?

Beatitude People do not confuse charity and justice. Many stand at the end of a tunnel where people emerge bleeding and battered and naked and homeless and without work, and offer bandages, clothing, houses, work and food. Which is excellent, but it is charity. Beatitude People are righteousness people. They tend to go up the tunnel to see who's hitting out, to inquire who's taking the clothes away. But there is a price to pay, because nobody wants you up there snooping around.

It is important to note that Beatitude People are persecuted *for righteousness' sake,* not for simply being obnoxious! The Early Church was persecuted and charged with

- *incest* (because they called one another 'brother and sister')
- *murder and cannibalism* (because they talked about eating and drinking Christ's body and blood)
- *sexual perversion* (because they met in groups, after dark)
- *atheism* (because they did not believe in the Roman gods)
- *disloyalty* (because they wouldn't worship Caesar or swear allegiance to him)
- *irreligion* (because they had no altars or temples) and
- *barbarians* (because they totally disregarded protocol and welcomed everyone of any social status equally).

But they were never accused of simply being obnoxious!

Overall, who do the Beatitudes most remind you of? As you begin to become a Beatitude Person who do you start to resemble? Jesus! Jesus, to whom the whole earth belonged, but who had nowhere to lay his head. Jesus, who had legions of angels available to him and yet

> *Beatitude People are Jesus-type people.*

died helplessly on a cross. Jesus, who rose from the dead declaring himself all-powerful over death, but who does not force a person to believe.

Beatitude People are willing to pay the price for the one they love

I recall visiting an old couple, married over 60 years. He was looking after her, and she was wizened, frail, skeletal, permanently in bed, near death. He ushered me upstairs to a tiny bedroom, sat on a small wicker chair next to the bed and held her hand. She opened her eyes. A pitiful sight, hardly any hair, no teeth, like an anorexic prune. He looked at me, and nodding at his wife as he squeezed her hand said, 'Isn't she lovely?'

Is it love or duty that lies at the heart of your continuing Christian discipleship?

You see, love sustains where duty won't. Ultimately the Beatitudes pose questions about our relationship with God. There, too, love will sustain where a sense of duty will not. To people long in the tooth in terms of church commitments, committee-going and sacrificial giving of time and money, the challenge of the Beatitudes – the challenge of the whole Sermon on the Mount – is whether love remains at the heart of our Christian discipleship.

For Beatitude People a continuing commitment based on love and gratitude, rather than a sense of duty or fear, sustains them. Which is another good reason why their picture is on God's wall!

FROM CHARACTER TO CONDUCT

(Matthew 5:17-48
– but don't read it yet!)

If the Beatitudes deal mainly with *character* then the remainder of Matthew 5 (and beyond) deals with different aspects of *conduct*. In teaching the Beatitudes Jesus does not ask his disciples to *do* anything much, but rather to *be* a certain kind of people. Jesus now continues on the basis that Beatitude People will *do* certain things as natural expressions of what they *are*.

This is the way of things throughout the Sermon on the Mount. A person's character determines their conduct rather than their conduct determining their character. (The same could be said about the Christian doctrine of sin: humans are not sinners because they sin; they sin because they are sinners.) What people *are* leads to what they *do*, rather than vice versa.

> **'What people are leads to what they do, rather than vice versa.' Yes or no?**

In this way Jesus regards character and conduct as closely connected. As Rob Warner in his book, *The Sermon on the Mount,* reminds us, Jesus strikes the balance between character and conduct. What you *are* is crucial, but what you are becomes evident in what you *do*, how you are, who you are. It's all of a piece.

Consequently, Jesus' teaching is at odds with those who focus on either character or conduct without the other. Those who focus on *conduct* in isolation from character finish up with legalism, with people whose lives and lips do not agree, with the kind of Pharisaism Jesus despised so much. Those who focus on *character* in isolation from conduct, usually finish up with an 'anything goes' attitude, with lawlessness. The Sermon on the Mount permits neither of these views.

> Before turning to read this demanding passage, spend some time in prayer. The words of a hymn by G. B. Caird, *Not far beyond the sea nor high above the heavens* (HP477) but found in many hymn books, may helpfully prepare you to study and receive God's word.
>
> Read Matthew 5:17-48. If you are in a group, allocate the several sections to different readers but read the *whole* passage at this point.

Note at this point that it consists of two main sections. In the first short section (vv 17-20) Jesus introduces the subject of the (Jewish) law. In the second, much longer section (vv21-48), Jesus gives six examples of what the law really means.

Activity – what do we make of it?

This is quite a passage of scripture! A group member once described it as a 'wow' passage. Another said, 'Not so much a wow passage as an 'oww' passage', because this was teaching so radical it hurt!

The radical nature of the teaching in the Sermon on the Mount, not least in this passage, has caused Christians down the ages to ask the question 'What do we make of it?' Before studying the passage in more detail, share what you 'make of it'. You may find it helpful to consider what other Christians have said . . .

Thomas Aquinas (the great medieval theologian) suggested that the teaching of the Sermon on the Mount was not intended for all Christians but only for a special category, namely the clergy!

Martin Luther (father of the Protestant Reformation) suggested that teaching such as this applies to 'Christ's kingdom', but not, in the same way, to 'the kingdom of this world'.

Some Lutherans have said it is impossible to obey the commands of Jesus in the Sermon on the Mount, but that that was not their real purpose. This teaching is deliberately impossible for two reasons: first, to make clear our own inadequacy and sinfulness causing us, secondly, to realise we must put our trust in Christ alone, rather than in our own ability to do God's will.

In the **19th century**, with its stress on individualism, some Christian thinkers suggested that what really counted was not so much the concrete obedience of these demands but the 'disposition of the heart'. In other words it was more important to feel right 'inside' than do right 'outside'.

Albert Schweitzer, among others, suggested that the Sermon on the Mount gave to Christians an 'interim ethic'. That is, this Sermon arises out of and relates to a period of time when the return of Jesus was expected imminently. In this intense time of expectation people could be expected to live out this highly demanding teaching. However, when Christ did not return as soon as was expected, the demands of the Sermon, while still authoritative, could not be regarded or applied in the same way.

Then there is the view which rumbles through Christian history, and which many affirm today, namely that according to Matthew, *Jesus actually expected all his followers to live according to these norms always and under all circumstances!*

Well, what do you make of it?

33

FULFILLING THE LAW
(Matthew 5:17-20)

Do not think that I have come to abolish the law or the prophets; I have not come to abolish but to fulfil. For truly I tell you, until heaven and earth pass away, not one letter, not one stroke of a letter, will pass from the law until all is accomplished. Therefore, whoever breaks one of the least of these commandments, and teaches others to do the same, will be called least in the kingdom of heaven; but whoever does them and teaches them will be called great in the kingdom of heaven. For I tell you, unless your righteousness exceeds that of the scribes and Pharisees, you will never enter the kingdom of heaven.

Do not think that I have come to abolish the law or the prophets; I have not come to abolish but to fulfil.

I bet they had to go round with smelling-salts on the mountainside at this point! This is a stunning claim, the most stupendous claim Jesus ever made, according to Martyn Lloyd-Jones. It is, note, the first time Jesus refers to himself in this Sermon. This is important, as the person and work of Jesus Christ is crucial to understanding this passage.

It may be that Jesus says, 'Do not think I have come to abolish the law' because that was just what some of his hearers were beginning to think. It may have dawned on them that to be a Beatitude Person did not seem to include the Jewish law – or put another way, these attributes and graces were possible without the Jewish law. If so, Jesus is going to put them straight!

What is the law that Jesus is to fulfil?

One way of answering this huge and complex question is to use the image of a marriage covenant, employed so helpfully by Mike Riddell in his book, *Threshold of the Future*.

When people love one another and intend to devote themselves to each other forever, they usually have a public ceremony to mark the fact. We call it marriage. Marriage means that the rights and responsibilities for both parties have changed. From the point of marriage the pair are bound together not only emotionally but also legally and morally and historically. They have covenanted to spend their lives together, and as a result they find new freedom in their relationship, but lay down certain other claims to freedom because of their commitment to each other.

The story of Israel in the Old Testament is essentially the story of a marriage covenant with God, and the Jewish law is the marriage agreement between God and God's

> *The Jewish law is the marriage agreement between God and God's chosen people.*

chosen people. So when Moses comes down a mountain with stone tablets in his arms, you are really looking at the wedding ring (a bit bulky perhaps, but a token of love and commitment nonetheless)!

Obedience to the law was Israel's side of the agreement, and the Old Testament provides an account of a sometimes rocky marriage owing to the fact that Israel keeps running after other partners, having 'affairs' and flouting the marriage. So much so that God nearly gives up on the relationship altogether on several occasions. Nearly, but not quite.

Whenever the marriage is going through rocky times, one thing always happens. The people go through the motions of the covenant, but their heart isn't in it. Like a wounded lover God has many heart-to-heart talks with them, often through chosen prophets. 'I want your steadfast love,' he tells them, 'not your empty sacrifices.' 'I want you to know me deeply,' he says, 'not offer me burnt offerings.'

There must have come a time when God decided that this 'formal agreement' with Israel wasn't working. All it seemed to do was drive a wedge between the actions of his people and the motivation that lay behind them. God wanted a living relationship with them, and they gave limp rituals. God wanted genuine faithfulness and they offered grim fasting.

So God sought a new way to create the kind of Covenant that he so desired. 'There will come a time,' God declared, 'when I will make a new marriage covenant with my people. Not like the old one which they kept breaking. No. This covenant I will place within them. I will write it on their hearts, not on tablets of stone. I will be their God and they will be my people.'

It is this kind of covenant relationship Jesus seems to have in mind as he teaches about the law. Which is one key reason why Jesus gives the Pharisees

> **The core of the law is found in the Ten Commandments.**
> **How do you regard these commandments viewed as a 'marriage agreement' between God and you?**

such a hard time! They emphasised the externals of religious behaviour whereas Jesus knew that the new, inner covenant lay in the heart, and nothing else would do.

What are we to make of the law?

The early Christians had to sort out a crucial issue and one central to our own discipleship today. It is this: what is the law you are going to live by?

As Christian disciples today it is important to note how adamant Jesus is that he is fulfilling rather than abolishing the law. And this law he is fulfilling, this law written on people's hearts, is not a different law to the 'old' law, but a completion of all the best intentions of that law.

There have always been Christians who see Jesus' teachings as a 'doing away' with the old law, superseding it, rendering it null and void. 'After all,' they say, 'we are Christians, and Christians are not Jews. We have left the law behind.' To such Christians it must be said that the teaching of Jesus does not permit such dismissing of the law. Nor, for that matter, does the teaching of Paul or the other early Christian writers. 'I am not going to abolish the law', says Jesus – and nor can we.

> **Read Galatians 3:19-26.**
>
> **How do you think Paul (a Jew and a Pharisee, remember) relates the Jewish law to faith in Christ? How do you relate the Jewish law to faith in Christ?**

Have you seen those tree protectors, little cylinders of plastic with holes in them? They help young trees to grow until the time they are strong enough to stand. Paul talks about the law in relation to faith in Christ in much the same way (Galatians 3:19-26). The law, Paul suggests, does not reconcile you to God, only Christ can do that, but it does help you until you become an heir, and you become an heir when you receive Christ. So when faith in Christ comes, the law has done its job, the 'tree protector' has fulfilled its purpose.

Jesus – the fulfilment of the law

Just as surely as Jesus claims that the law cannot be abolished, he is equally clear that he is fulfilling it. For all its God givenness, the law is *incomplete*.

R. T. Kendall suggests that the Jewish law 'was but a parenthesis in salvation history'. Parentheses are brackets in a sentence, and whatever falls inside brackets in a sentence can be left out without changing the meaning of the sentence, even though what is in brackets may make the precise meaning of the sentence clearer. So when Jesus says he is the fulfilment of the law, he effectively marks the end of 1300-year-old brackets. He is really saying, 'I am the fulfilment of the Old Testament'! No wonder some of the Jewish hearers needed smelling-salts!

> Moses gave the Law, but couldn't fulfil it. Joshua perpetuated the Law (Joshua 1:8) but couldn't satisfy its demands. King David loved the Law (Psalm 119:163) but broke it. The prophets upheld the Law, but couldn't keep it as required. The Levites carried out the Law, but they still came short of it. The Pharisees and Sadducees and teachers of the Law argued about it but didn't have a clue as to its deeper meaning. But the very Messiah they rejected was the prophet Moses spoke of (Deuteronomy 18:15; Acts 3:22).
>
> R. T. Kendall

We draw near to the very heart of the Christian gospel. Only the Messiah could fulfil the law. And in so doing – in fulfilling the law, which we could never do – he takes our place under the law – God in Christ brought about salvation and life through suffering and dying.

Donald English often used this illustration.

Have you ever spilt ink on a new carpet? Worse still, have you ever spilt ink on someone else's new carpet? If so, imagine if you had a piece of blotting-paper which, when laid on the carpet, sucked out all the stain, leaving the carpet like new. Wonderful! Imagine how much blotting-paper like that you could sell. You'd be rich. But imagine you had a piece of blotting-paper that sucked out all the stain and when you turned it over the paper itself was clean. Then you wouldn't be rich, because everyone would only ever need one piece!

Then Donald would pause and say, 'And once, for all, Christ died for us.'

The new covenant is begun through the life and death and resurrection of Jesus himself. In his life he exemplifies the law. In his death he fulfils the law. As the resurrected Lord he fills his disciples with his Spirit. The law has become written not on tablets of stone, but in human hearts. That is the New Law under which we live. It is a gift of God, fulfilled in Christ and sustained by the Holy Spirit. We didn't earn it. We can't buy it. It's gospel, quite literally good news. Do you know that? If you don't know that you may have just joined the Pharisees!

In what ways is the gospel 'good news' in your life?

To whom we now turn.

> *Unless your righteousness surpasses that of the Scribes and Pharisees you will never enter the kingdom of heaven*
>
> (Matthew 5:20)

Another statement from Jesus resulting in more smelling-salts – or possibly oxygen masks – being distributed on the mountainside.

More righteous than the Pharisees! Impossible! It's like being told you need to be better at football than Michael

Owen or better at golf than Tiger Woods! The Pharisees were walking law machines, professional interpreters of the law. They were known as the 'righteous' ones. They sorted out the law – the Torah as it is often known – into over 600 rules. Then they added over 1500 emendations to them, effectively putting a fence round the inner sanctum of the 600 rules. Only by keeping the law perfectly, they taught, could a person please God, and expect the coming of the Messiah.

Jesus' hearers on the hillside must have wondered whether there *could* be righteousness greater than that of the Pharisees. But even more seriously, Jesus said *unless* you have such righteousness, you will not enter the kingdom of God! It is not that you won't become a bigwig in the kingdom, it is that you won't even get in! I wonder whether some got up and wandered disconsolately down the mountainside at this point?

THE LAW OF GOD – JESUS STYLE
(Matthew 5:21-48)

Having dropped this bombshell, Jesus proceeds to give them six examples of what he means by righteousness that goes beyond that of the Pharisees. Each example follows a similar pattern: Jesus takes a statement from the Ten Commandments, or from other parts of the Old Testament and Jewish tradition, and then adds a repeated mind-blowing statement. He says:

You have heard it said . . . but I say to you

Try to put yourself in the place of those Jewish hearers.

Often what follows 'You have heard it said' is a statement of Mosaic law which every Jew knew had been given by God, so can you feel the shock of a statement which means, in effect, 'You know what God has said . . . But I say to you'!

Pass the smelling-salts again!

But those looking for disagreement between God and Jesus will not find it here. It is not so much that Jesus revises the law, or alters it; it would be more accurate to say that he interprets it so that its real meaning becomes plainer than ever before. He presents the law *as God understands it.*

Below the surface of the law

In each of these six examples Jesus goes *underneath* the surface of the law to its deeper meaning.

We've had trouble with our little house recently. Cracks appeared on two outside walls, and the whole side of the house began to have a sort of 'leaned over' sad look. A man came and looked at it and said, 'We're going to have to dig little holes in the garden.' I said, 'The garden's fine, it's the wall. Just fix the wall.' 'No,' he said. 'The walls have gone like that because the pipe in the garden's collapsed. It's no use fixing the wall till the pipe's mended.'

I was looking at the symptoms; the contractor was identifying the *cause.*

In this teaching Jesus is concerned first with the cause, and then with the symptoms. It's like looking in a pond. Sometimes the light bounces off the surface and you can't see below the water at all. Other times the light enables you to see the depths of the water. That's what Jesus does here. He sheds light on the depth of God's law.

Windows and mirrors

Jesus takes tablets of stone, which you can't see through, and makes them a window, so we can see what God is like.

Or again, Jesus takes tablets of stone and makes them into a mirror, so we can see ourselves in the light of what God is like.

He goes behind the flat statements of ritual religion and says, 'Now what are your *attitudes* in these matters?' Jesus is calling us away from righteousness long on theology and short on charity, strong on the nouns of the Christian faith and weak on the verbs. He is calling us towards a righteousness that springs from our hearts and into action. This is what Jesus means by righteousness more truly righteous than that of the Pharisees, a righteousness where what is 'inside' leads naturally to what is 'outside'.

Whole of life discipleship

> *If Jesus is not Lord of all, he isn't Lord at all.*

Jesus is really talking about whole of life discipleship. What he really despises about the Pharisees is their split-level living. They did not practise what they preached because what was inside was different to what was paraded outside. 'Whitewashed tombs' Jesus called them. Clean on the outside, dead and decaying on the inside. Champions of the law, but ironically those who came to hate everything Jesus, the fulfiller of the law they sought to preserve, stood for. Creators of laws that ran contrary to the deeper covenantal law of God: 'You mustn't heal on the Sabbath . . . you ought to keep better company . . .'

In what ways are we like the Pharisees? What would it mean for us to move towards the kind of righteousness Jesus urges here?

SSD Syndrome

Mark Greene of the London Institute for Contemporary Christianity talks about SSD Syndrome as the greatest and most common challenge facing the Church today. SSD is *Sacred-Secular Divide* Syndrome – 'the pervasive belief that some parts of our life aren't really important to God'. This virus-like, tough to cure condition is suffered by almost every Christian at one time or another and its chief symptom is the compartmentalising of faith in our lives.

- When we think that our Christianity is something we believe but not do, or do but not believe
- When we live in two worlds, the world of church and the 'normal' world
- When we pretend that prayers, church services and church-based activities concern discipleship, and work, school and leisure aren't really part of this discipleship thing at all
- When we separate Jesus as Saviour and Jesus as Lord in our thinking

we are suffering from SSD Syndrome.

The technical term for this is dualism. We

SSD Syndrome – Have you got it?

split up what belongs together. Jesus says, the righteousness I'm talking about is all of a piece. Is ours, or are we suffering from SSD?

A good method of diagnosing how badly you've contracted SSD Syndrome is gauging how you relate and respond to the six examples of the new righteousness Jesus provides.

Read these short sections again, one by one, and permit time for sharing. Be especially sensitive to each other, and commit yourself to careful listening with respect, as these are sensitive issues.

Anger (vv21-26)

Jesus says, it's not only murder, it's anger – be angry like this, and you are guilty before God.

> *If you have been part of a local church for more than six months, and nobody has irritated you yet, then you're probably clinically dead.*
>
> Jeff Lucas

- Watch your words (the person who said, 'Sticks and stones may break my bones but words can never hurt me' didn't know what he was talking about!)
- Seek and take initiatives for reconciliation
- Try fervently to prevent escalation of tension.

Lust (vv27-30)

Jesus says it's not only adultery (by which the Pharisees meant the *act* of adultery), it's lusting – lusting is guilt before God.

King of the hill, the Study Guide for Spring Harvest 2001 urges a rejection of 'Victorian prudishness' in favour of honouring and celebrating 'the wonderful gift of sexuality in the liberating context of covenant-marriage'. In pursuit of this, Christian disciples are *called away from*:

Sexual superficiality (where people are regarded as 'objects' and sex is separated from love.)

A lack of self-awareness ('If your eye causes you to sin,' says Jesus, 'cut it out', implying we should have the self-awareness to know whether or not it does.)

Self-deception (Lust has a powerful habit of enabling our minds to rationalise and fantasise: 'We're only friends . . . God is bringing us together . . . after all, everyone is doing it . . .')

Costless Christianity (In direct contrast to a 'just do it' culture Jesus urges us to take responsibility for our sexuality and will and work for those right choices, praying and seeking God's help and grace.)

Divorce (vv31-32)

Divorce was easy in Jesus' day. Burn the dinner and the husband (note, not the wife) only had to say, 'I divorce you.

> **Link:** *Jesus provides fuller teaching on this issue in Matthew 19:1-12.*

I divorce you. I divorce you.' And that was that! Some say that by permitting divorce on any grounds, Jesus is making it too easy. The main point of this teaching, however, is not so much about easy divorce as guarding marriage. The key issue is not so much the means whereby you can get a bill of divorce but whether you are honouring marriage as given by God.

Some have pointed out that in this teaching Jesus upheld the rights of legally discarded women. Certainly men who divorce their wives for trivial reasons find little sympathy here.

Oaths (vv33-37)

Jesus says it's not only about oaths – the teachers of the law had worked out which oaths needed to be kept and which didn't – it's about verbal integrity. Your 'yes' and your 'no' will do – if you are a truthful person.

> *The ideal society is one in which no person will ever need an oath to guarantee its truth, and no one's promise ever need an oath to guarantee its fulfilling.*
>
> Clement of Alexandria c.AD200

Retaliation (vv38-42)

You have heard that it was said, 'An eye for an eye . . .'
But I say to you . . .

Jesus says, not just one cheek but both, not just your cloak but also your coat, not just one mile, but two. Dynamite!

Revenge and response

Here Jesus begins to talk not about *revenge* but *response*. Originally, the Mosaic law was given not to make the punishment as *severe* as possible but as *reasonable* as possible. It was given so that a life would not be taken for a tooth, or a heart for an eye. The law was given to define the maximum legitimate punishment, and that was based on the principle of equivalence.

But over time, as is the human way with these things, this teaching had come to mean, insist on as much punishment as you can, get as much as you can squeeze, very much like certain sorts of legal adverts today urging you to sue and make claims.

What Jesus is getting at here is very important. He says, don't *react* against wrongdoing; *respond* to it. Simple reaction gives wrongdoing much of its power: she does this, he does that, so she does the other. Asserts Jesus, if you *respond* to wrongdoing in a certain way you can empty it of its power.

If someone hits you on the right cheek, says Jesus, with the most insulting hit they can – and in Jewish culture it was the backhander that was the real insult (and if you are right-handed there is no way of hitting someone on the right cheek except as a backhander) – offering the other cheek empties the insult of its offence.

If someone asks you for your tunic, says Jesus, give her your cloak also. (Remember the cloak was the peasant's most valuable piece of clothing, it covered her by day and was a blanket by night.) It is as if Jesus says, 'Don't allow them the power of demanding from you; offer them something. By giving your cloak the demand is emptied of its power.'

If anyone forces you to go a mile (and by Roman law a Jew could be forced by a Roman soldier to carry his pack one mile) Jesus says, 'Don't get worked up about it. Don't curse them under your breath in Aramaic. Carry the pack until the first mile is up, and say, "Now, would you like me to walk another mile?"'

> How do you respond to this teaching of Jesus? How does it make you feel?

Impossible teaching?

Some of us get angry at such teaching. 'Impossible!' we say. 'It's just not practical. Jesus wouldn't say that if he was in my situation . . . or if he knew what I know . . .' But then Jesus practised exactly what he preached. It is with a crown of thorns on his head and nails through his hands and feet that he prays for his torturers. Nor is Jesus giving such teaching in a cosy palace in a peaceful time. He is in the midst of Roman occupation and oppression. He knows what he's asking. This is no 'academic' teaching.

We need to note that such 'impossible teaching' is not academic for many Christians today, but is intensely practical. 'How far would you like us to go?' is said by Christians the world over. In many contexts today Christians walk like clowns through the world, and keep the gospel by saying, 'You demand a mile, here's two'; 'You take a coat, here's a cloak'; 'You want to hit this cheek, here's this one as well.' So much so that some oppressors of the Church today say, as they did of the earliest Christians, 'What do we do with these people?'

We need to support these, our sisters and brothers in Christ. We need to support them practically, politically and prayerfully. As so many of us lie in our cosy beds, no tanks rumbling through the streets, nobody hammering on our door in the dead of night, I hope we can hear their voices. They shame us, they heap hot coals on our heads when we rationalise this teaching, and say it is too hard.

Because that is what God is like!

There is another reason why Christian disciples must take such 'impossible' teaching with the utmost seriousness. Turning the other cheek, going the second mile, loving enemies are to be undertaken because God is like that! God is gracious to the undeserving, the selfish; God makes the sun to shine on the just and unjust alike. The theme of universal love lies deep in this teaching. Jesus is saying, 'If God can love 'em, why can't you love 'em?' Why love your enemies? Because that is what God is like, and disciples of Jesus will want to be like that.

Have you ever seen selective sunshine, shining only on the righteous and warming them through? Have you ever seen raindrops, like guided missiles, targeting unrighteous people? The sun comes out and everyone feels its warmth. The rain falls and everyone gets wet. Jesus says, 'If God provides for the just and the unjust – why can't you?'

Habits of the heart

Which 'habit of the heart' is the first step towards a more whole life Christian discipleship for you?

Christian discipleship, then, is not primarily adherence to a legal or ethical code. It is a relational living faith in Jesus Christ from which *a whole life discipleship naturally emerges*. The righteousness greater than that of the Pharisees Jesus speaks of is really the habits of the heart of Christian disciples working themselves out quite naturally. They are not *easy* – but they are *possible*.

Be perfect, therefore, as your Father in heaven is perfect

(Matthew 5:48)

Time for a final bout of smelling-salts for those folk still conscious on the mountain!

> *I can't help but believe that this statement came straight from Jesus. No thinking human would have written such a statement off their own back!*
>
> Donald English

What does it mean to be perfect AS GOD IS perfect? One thing it may well mean is being perfect in relation to our *loving*.

Perfect love

Perfect love – or loving – is one of the jewels in the Methodist spiritual treasure chest. John Wesley talked about perfect love, with the result that holiness is important to Methodists. Holiness, for Wesley, was not simply about how many sins you've committed today, or how many you've not. Holiness is not primarily about computers keeping a 'sin tally' in heaven, nor does it work like 'goal difference'. Holiness is more about the extent to which God's love has filled your being.

Wesley implies that if you are filled with love it doesn't altogether matter if you don't altogether get it right. Theologically he was skating on pretty thin ice; biblically and pastorally he had it dead right! God is more concerned that our lives be filled with love than that we get it right all the time. (Who wants to live with someone who gets it right all the time, anyway?)

The key truth of Christian perfection lies not in behaviour but in *identity*. Perfection and piety become portable in Christian disciples because their identity is one who is 'in

Perfection and piety become portable in Christian disciples because their identity is one who is 'in Christ'.

Christ'. You'll never live by law. Try it and you'll make a fool of yourself. But try to live by love, and you'll find it is possible – hard, but possible. What is 'inside' will work 'outside' quite naturally.

How then do we live? Grace and demand

In this part of the Sermon, then, Jesus teaches two absolutes: the absolute ideals of God, and the absolute grace of God on which we can rely and in which is our hope.

The first absolute – the ideals of God – will probably have left us uneasy. Who has not thought at some point in this study, 'If these are God's standards, I've had it from the start'? Sometimes this teaching of Jesus has condemned us and we know it. The recognition and acceptance that we will never measure up is, however, a proper starting point, and far from being a negative factor is a very positive realisation. Because, you see, we don't have to measure up. We are judged by the righteousness of Christ who lives within, not our own righteousness. God always matches demand and grace. That is Good News!

As Christian disciples we live within the God-given tension of these two absolutes. Anytime we dare to think, 'I've got it sussed' in respect of

> **The absolute ideals of God, and the absolute grace of God. Are you 'in balance', or do you need to come into balance?**

Christ's standards we are deceiving ourselves. But equally, anytime we feel unable to trust and believe in God's gracious forgiving love, we are deceiving ourselves. As Philip Yancey puts it, 'Having fallen from the absolute Ideal, we have nowhere to land but in the safety net of absolute grace.' Praise God, that net will never let us slip through!

Some years ago, when computers were as big as a bus, the *National Geographic* magazine computer which sent reminders when subscriptions lapsed broke and sent 9,416 identical reminders to a sheep herder in the wilds of Kansas. The first he knew of it was when a large mail truck came down the dusty track, turned into his ranch, and a mailman deposited three large sacks of mail at his porch door, then drove away.

He opened one, then another, then another, then a few more – just to see if they were all the same. He opened the other two sacks and tried a few more – they were all the same.

He threw the sacks into his truck, leapt into it and roared up the track heading to the town several miles away where the nearest mail office was located. There he went inside and wired a telegraph to *National Geographic* magazine. It consisted of just six words. 'I give in (stop). Renew my subscription (stop).'

Faced with such challenges, offered such grace, it may be time for us to renew our subscription!

A prayer for starters . . . no doubt you will want to add prayers of your own.

> Idealistic, gracious God,
> I don't want to break our relationship,
> I want to live as a Christian disciple however hard
>   its demands,
> because however hard its demands,
> this relationship of hard love
> is where I want to be,
> where I need to be
> and where through grace I can be.
> Thank you, Lord. Amen.

PRACTICES, PRIORITIES & PROMISES – CHRISTIAN SPIRITUALITY

(Matthew 6)

Read Matthew 6. If you are in a group, allocate the several sections to different readers but read the *whole* chapter at this point. Assuming that all the material relating to chapter 6 is not studied in one meeting, you may want to read chapter 6 at the start of each meeting dealing with this material.

Overview

Jesus turns his attention to the kind of *spirituality* Christian discipleship demands. We are going to deal with the material in this chapter in three main sections, the first being longer than the others.

- Section one (6:1-18) concerns *practices*, in particular the religious practices of giving, praying and fasting.
- Section two (6:19-24) concerns *priorities*, particularly in relation to 'treasure' and 'service'.
- Section three (6:25-34) concerns God's *promises*, leading to Jesus' mind-blowing instruction that disciples are not to worry or be anxious.

Taken together, a person's religious practices, priorities and responses to God's promises produce their spirituality. Jesus makes it clear that those seeking God's kingdom above everything else will be people with a certain kind of spirituality, a 'living spirituality', sourced and shaped by God in the life of a willing disciple.

SECTION ONE
RELIGIOUS PRACTICES AND SPIRITUAL PEOPLE
(Matthew 6:1-18)

Some of us will find this teaching of Jesus even more sharp and challenging than the teaching in chapter 5. Chapter 5 painted a picture of a Beatitude Person, one who in many important respects did not conform to 'the world'. Though extremely challenging, this teaching is grist to the mill to those who know that to be a Christian disciple is to be different, to march to a different drum to the rest of society. You may have found that some group members readily jumped on to world-rejecting soapboxes when discussing this material.

Doing religion differently

Here, in chapter 6, Jesus moves closer to home for many of us, because he teaches about doing religion differently, about not conforming to the *religious* establishment. We will have noted, as religious people, that Jesus has as hard and as radical things to say about wrong religion as he does about wrong character or wrong morality or wrong society. In this teaching Jesus puts our 'religious righteousness' under the spotlight.

Giving, praying, fasting

Jesus focuses upon the three main religious practices that characterised Judaism: giving, praying and fasting.

These three religious practices represent different aspects of spirituality.

Giving mainly concerns your dealings with *others*,
Prayer mainly concerns your dealings with *God* and
Fasting mainly concerns your dealings with *yourself*.

Get these right and you are well on the way to a rounded, mature spirituality. So bubbling under the surface of this section of the Sermon are the questions 'How's your spirituality? How are your dealings with God, with others, and with yourself?'

Sort these things out, suggests Jesus, and the later questions of priorities and worry almost take care of themselves.

Not whether, but how

It is worth noting that in each case the issue is not *whether* you give or pray or fast – Jesus just assumes that disciples do (do you?) – but *how* you go about giving or praying or fasting. As we found in earlier teaching, the *motives* behind the religious practices are crucial. Jesus is primarily concerned with *how* these religious practices are observed in terms of inward spirit rather than simply outward action. Here is another example of what's inside working itself out, rather than vice versa.

> **Share with each other, openly and honestly, *whether* you give, pray and fast, and if you do, your motives for doing so. The group is pledged to listen and encourage rather than judge.**

Hypocrisy

Beware of practising your piety before others in order to be seen by them; for then you have no reward from your Father in heaven.

So whenever you give alms, do not sound a trumpet before you, as the hypocrites do in the synagogues and, at the street corners, so that they may be seen by others. Truly I tell you, they have received their reward . . .

And whenever you pray, do not be like the hypocrites; for they love to stand and pray in the synagogues and in the streets, so that they may be praised by others. Truly I tell you, they have received their reward . . .

And whenever you fast, do not look dismal, like the hypocrites, for they disfigure their faces so as to show others that they are fasting. Truly I tell you, they have received their reward . . .

(selected verses from Matthew 6:1-16)

We really have to come to terms with hypocrisy. In each case – giving, praying, fasting – Jesus begins with a negative rather than a positive command: 'Do not be like the hypocrites.' He doesn't say, 'Do it like this', he says, 'Don't do it like them!'

Most of us will have a good idea of what a hypocrite is; in fact, we ought to note that it was mainly Jesus who gave the term the morally dubious connotations we now so often associate with it. But we ought also to look at the origins of the word. The term 'hypocrite' comes from Greek and particularly the world of theatre. It denotes someone wearing a mask in order to cover up his or her true feelings. A hypocrite is someone acting, playing out a part. Jesus may be saying, in effect, 'Stop acting, stop playing a part. When you give or pray or fast, let it be real.'

Jesus also suggests that hypocrites will get the reward they seek, but nothing else. Actors play to the audience. If they do well they receive applause. Applause is the right reward for a performance, but that is the sum of it. Jesus is saying to those who act at giving or praying or fasting, 'You wanted people to see and hear you. They have. You have what you wanted. You've had your reward. Nothing more is owed, or deserved.' Instead Jesus suggests that nobody needs to see what you give, or when you pray or fast. If you do it for 'show' God will write 'Paid, nothing more owed' across it. That God 'sees' these religious practices is the only significant thing, and that brings a different reward.

> **For discussion . . .**
> *Whenever you pray, go into your room and shut the door and pray to your Father who is in secret; and your Father who sees in secret will reward you.*
> (Matthew 6:6-7)
>
> *Let your light so shine that they may see your good works.* (Matthew 5:16)
>
> **How do these two pieces of teaching relate to each other?**

My own view is that I don't think Jesus means that disciples should not pray together. This isn't a command not to pray with others, it is a command not to pray *in order to be seen by others.*

Similarly, Jesus is not saying, 'Don't give' but 'Don't give *in order* to be seen to give.' He is not saying 'Don't fast', he is saying 'Fast, but don't look like the religious people when you do it.'

Jesus does not say, 'Don't practise your piety before others', he says, 'Beware of practising your piety before *others in order to be seen by them.'*

Nearly all 'acts of righteousness' are 'before others', but it is the *motive* that is crucial. They are not done so you can pat yourself on the back, or done to win the applause or admiration of others. They are done before God.

Who is it for?

The hypocrisy issue then, leads to a key question – 'Who is it all for?'

> **Is your giving or praying or fasting based on a desire to be popular? Or is it to please God?**

Jesus suggests that giving and praying and fasting is undertaken for an 'audience' of one – God!

It was said of the Puritans that they 'lived their lives as if stood before an audience of one', as if the only person who mattered was God. It is really a question of *approval*. For whose approval is this done? We do not worship in order for people to see us, but in order to offer worship to God. The important thing is 'What does God think of us?'

Hiders and seekers

Throughout this passage Jesus makes one other rather disturbing thing clear, that being 'religious', and doing all the right things, is not enough.

Let us dare to rehearse a couple of home truths at this point.

- Some folk want to appear religious, without really wanting *God*.
- Some folk deliberately appear religious in order to *escape* meeting God.

> *We structure our churches and maintain them so as to shield us from God and protect us from genuine religious experience.*
>
> Clyde Reid

Is that actually true of us? If so, is it time to take the mask off, stop playing the part, and get real with God? Be assured, God can stand the shock!

There are, in the end, only two groups of people, hiders and seekers, those who hide from God, and those who seek God. Which are we?

Most of us will have played 'hide and seek' at some time or other. Have you ever found a hiding-

> *Time to be found?*

place so good that you said to yourself as you hid, 'Nobody will ever find me here'? If so, you may have had the experience of realising after a while, 'I'm right, nobody *is* ever going to find me here!' So what do you do? Slowly but surely you make your hiding-place known. You cough loudly as the seekers come near. Or if that doesn't work eventually you emerge from your hiding-place and shout, 'Coo-eee, I'm here!' Because, in the end, there is a deep need in humans to be found. And the wonderful thing is that God – Father, Son and Spirit – is seeking you, and never ceases seeking you.

How's your giving going?

Whenever you give alms, do not sound a trumpet before you, as the hypocrites do . . . so that they may be praised by others . . . But when you give alms, do not let your left hand know what your right hand is doing, so that your alms may be done in secret; and your Father who sees in secret will reward you.

(Matthew 6:2-4)

In his hilarious 'half-hour' *The Blood Donor*, Tony Hancock speaks for many of us:

> I always give what I can . . . Have a look at this. It's all in me diary. Congo Relief, two-and-six, Self-Denial Week, one-and-eight, Lifeboat Day, sixpence . . . Yes, it's all down here. Yes, yes, I do what I can, my conscience is clear. And when I'm finally called, by the great architect, and he says, 'What did you do?' I shall just bring me book out and I shall say, 'Here you are, mate, add that lot up!'

But the kind of giving Jesus is talking about seems to have as much to do with a person's *own* goodness as the merits or demerits of the people or causes to which they give.

> The Christian Aid collector knocked on the grubby front door and waited. She was just about to turn away when the door opened and a man appeared. She explained what she was collecting for. He listened, then in broken English said, 'I'm sorry, we have no money, will you receive some of our vouchers?' He was an asylum seeker.

Not knowing your right hand from your left

When you give alms, do not let your left hand know what your right hand is doing . . .

(Matthew 6:3)

Discuss together what you think this means.

For example (someone might like to act this out?):

Usually I put one hand into my pocket, pull out all the money in it, open my hand, and then sort out the money with the fingers of my other hand. The second hand effectively counts the money and aids me make a mental record of how much there is. I then count out an amount, lift it out of my open hand with the fingers of my second hand and replace the remaining money in my pocket with my first hand.

But if I were simply to put my hand into my pocket and pull out the money and then give it I would not know how much was there.

Is that what Jesus means?

If so, is this the way we should be dealing with our brothers and sisters in the World Church? Perhaps we have to say, 'We have given the money, now you [in South America, Africa, or wherever] decide what to do with it'? Losing power takes risks. True giving inevitably involves risks.

Is that what Jesus means?

Does it mean that we give automatically, unconsciously, without thinking? You don't say to yourself, 'Now the right foot, now the left' when you want to walk somewhere!

Is that how Jesus wants us to give?
If so, how's your giving going?

How's your praying going?

An 'inner place':

Whenever you pray, go to your room and shut the door and pray to your Father . . .

(Matthew 6:6)

Jesus suggests that there is something intimate about prayer. If this intimacy is to flourish there is a need to find 'an inner place' to pray.

Can you imagine if every conversation between you and those closest to you took place in public – even 'Big Brother'

doesn't do that! You see, our deepest relationships are those that are not played out in public, and it is the intimate secret places that sustain relationships. So, says Jesus, make sure there is an 'inner place' for your praying.

For some of us this prayer thing is very difficult. I recall the story of a priest who went to his bishop and related how hard it was to pray at all. The bishop said, 'Go home, settle yourself, then pray, "Lord, make me want what you want." ' 'I've tried that, I can't,' replied the priest. 'In that case,' said the bishop, 'pray first "Lord, make me want to want what you want" and keep at it, and see what happens.' That may be a word for some of us.

The Lord's Prayer

When you are praying, do not heap up empty phrases as the Gentiles do; for they think that they will be heard because of their many words. Do not be like them, for your Father knows what you need before you ask him.

Pray then in this way:

Our Father in heaven,
hallowed be your name.
Your kingdom come.
Your will be done,
        on earth as it is in heaven.
Give us this day our daily bread.
And forgive us our debts,
        as we also have forgiven our debtors.
And do not bring us to the time of trial,
        but rescue us from the evil one.

For if you forgive others their trespasses, your heavenly Father will also forgive you; but if you do not forgive others, neither will your Father forgive your trespasses.

(Matthew 6:7-15)

A lengthy look at the Lord's Prayer constitutes another study guide booklet and is beyond the scope of this one. A couple of observations must suffice.

How do you view God?

Pray then in this way: Our Father . . .

How you pray reveals how you view God. When some folk pray it is clear that God is regarded as a sort of divine vending-machine dispensing this and that. Many pray as if God is the landlord and they are the tenants – 'Please put the plumbing right, Lord!'

How we view God is actually very important to how we pray. Here is a silly example making a serious point. Perhaps one member of the group could read it 'dramatically' while the rest of the group close their eyes and imagine . . ?

Imagine you are at school and are unexpectedly summoned to the headmaster's office. Now you know that the headmaster is a child-hating monster! You start to quiver and your heart beats faster. You slowly leave the classroom, think about running home, decide against it, and then even more slowly make your way down the long corridors to his office. Despite this dawdling it seems no time at all before you stand at his door. You tap it as lightly as you dare, praying that he isn't in. But a split second after you knock, the door flies open, a big hairy arm reaches out and lifts you clean off your feet and dumps you in a chair. Then an awful voice shouts, 'What have you been doing in my school . . !'

But now imagine that you are at school and are unexpectedly summoned to the (let's be sexist and stereotypical!) headmistress's office. Now you know that the headmistress is sweetness and light and loves children. There is no thought of running home, and no racing heartbeats. You stroll down the corridor, perhaps even pop into the 'loo' for a quick smoke or hairbrush, and on arriving at her office door knock confidently. She opens the door and greets you with a smile, she shows you to a seat, offers you a sweet, then says soothingly, 'Now tell me, what has the wicked world been doing to you?'

Two silly, imaginary scenarios. Yet all the responses in both cases are determined almost completely by the kind of person you believe you are going to find behind that office door.

Share with one another: how do you view the God to whom you pray?

Here in the Lord's Prayer, as so often in the Sermon on the Mount, Jesus reminds his hearers of something awesome: the relationship of discipleship is between heavenly parent and loved child. Hence 'Our Father'.

I've come to notice in recent years that those folk who have really focused on an 'angry God' in terms of atonement theory, have quite a lot of difficulty being children of God. I am not arguing against such atonement theories altogether, but it does seem peculiar to hold to a view which seems to set God and Jesus over against each other when Jesus flatly refuses to do that in his deepest teaching.

How do our views of 'atonement' influence our view of God?

Availability, reliance and obedience

What else might we note about this prayer of Jesus?

It is a prayer about *availability* to God. People who truly pray the Lord's Prayer do so not in order to 'use' God – the 'give us' mentality – but to be used by God.

It is a prayer about *reliance* upon God. There is a 'one day at a time' quality laid deep in this prayer, which is, of course, the slogan for addicts of many kinds. Those folk undergoing rehabilitation for addictions of alcohol, gambling, smoking, illegal drugs and the like all know the importance and significance of 'one day at a time'. 'Father, give us this day' is the slogan for Christian disciples.

It is a prayer about *obedience* to God. The prayer is essentially about God in charge. The disciple states as she prays, 'God, it is *your* will which prevails in my life.'

> **Share with one another the significance and importance of the Lord's Prayer in your own life.**

Known by heart?

In your discussions you probably mentioned the effect that repeating the Lord's Prayer hundreds, possibly thousands, of times has upon you. For some familiarity will sadly have bred contempt. I want to urge us to realise what a gift it is to know something by heart. Did you note that phrase? *Known by heart.*

There is a world of difference between merely repeating things and knowing things by heart. The Lord's Prayer is not 'groan' or 'switch off' time in an act of worship, it is the *Lord's* Prayer, a gift to his disciples, an insight into his own spirituality.

When Terry Waite was released from captivity, after more than three years held 'hostage' in Beirut, and stood, thinner

and greyer on that RAF base tarmac, I remember clearly his answer to the question 'How did you keep sane, how did you survive?' He said, 'I recited the morning and evening prayer offices to myself each day.' Now, he had no prayer book. But he didn't need one. He knew those prayers by heart. And it kept him alive.

Truly to know something by heart is to place it at the core of your being. Do you recite the Lord's Prayer, or do you know it by heart?

How's your praying going?

Suggestion

It may be appropriate that a time of prayer conclude this session. Responding positively and sensitively to those who find it hard to pray, who have shared a concern, who seek a deeper prayer life, is vital. Try to ensure that nobody leaves without them feeling affirmed and supported in prayer.

How's your fasting going?

Share with each other –
do we fast?

If so, why, and what are
the benefits?

If not, why is that?

As always, listen hard
and be sensitive.

*And whenever you fast, do
not look dismal, like the
hypocrites . . . But when
you fast, put oil on your
head and wash your face,
so that your fasting may
be seen not by others but
by your Father . . .*

(Matthew 6:16-18)

You may have seen them. Long faces, unwashed hair, perhaps a stubbly beard, pressing microphones to their stomach to magnify the rumbling! Acting out the part of 'the faster'. And everyone is supposed to say, 'Oh, look at them, they're giving up so much, you know . . .'

What is fasting all about? Is it really about how 'religious' and 'long-suffering' you look? Jesus suggests not and in some ways takes us back to the origins of fasting.

Originally fasting was not primarily about doing without food. The 'giving up food' bit emerged naturally when you were in a state when you 'couldn't eat a thing'. Fasting is therefore originally associated with times of deep emotion, seeking, upset, anguish or trial, times leaving a person with no appetite. It was at such times that folk sought God, inner peace, got to grips with themselves, assessed the situation, thought things through, resolved some sort of action. Fasting, then, demonstrates what you are committed to, what you are seriously exercised about.

Asceticism

Fasting has also always been associated with asceticism and, put simply, asceticism is the business of saying 'no' to yourself. Fasting is a contemporary expression of asceticism. By fasting a disciple says to God, 'I can't live without your nourishment.' At its best fasting is more about denial of self than self-denial. There is a difference between self-denial and denial of self. Self-denial can actually be self-congratulatory. Denial of self can't. Some of us need to diet in 'me' making! The best fasting is rooted in denial of self and seeking of God.

'Enoughness'

The Archbishop of York recently told his clergy that Christians badly need to develop a theology of 'enoughness'. Our consumer driven culture is not used to the idea of 'enoughness', and far more used to the sentiments expressed by the McDonald's strap-line 'Enjoy More'. To say, 'Enough' – I have enough – is a counter-cultural thing. And yet 'enoughness' bubbles under the surface of this teaching and is therefore a proper question for Christian 'fasters' to consider.

How's your fasting going?

The issue of 'rewards'

. . . and your Father who sees in secret will reward you.

Three times Jesus mentions it. Get your giving right, praying right and fasting right and God who sees in secret will reward you. Some people are 'iffy' about the notion of rewards. Does it demean the action, sully the intention? I go with C. S. Lewis:

We must not be troubled by unbelievers when they say that this promise of reward makes the Christian life a mercenary affair. There are different kinds of rewards. There is the reward which has no natural connection with the things you do to earn it and is quite foreign to the desires that ought to accompany those things. Money is not the natural reward of love; that is why we call a man mercenary if he marries a woman for the sake of her money. But marriage is the proper reward for a real lover, and he is not mercenary for desiring it . . . The proper rewards are not simply tacked on to the activity for which they are given, but are the activity itself in consummation.

Indulging in a little heresy!

Before we leave this section of the Sermon on the Mount, let's indulge in a little dangerous thinking, a little 'heresy'. In each case of religious practice – giving, praying, and fasting – Jesus is adamant that his disciples are not to conform to the 'religious establishment' of the day. What might 'not conforming to the religious establishment' mean for us today?

It almost certainly means that we reject the worldliness and nominality of the Church in whatever form it takes. It probably means that we are right to be discontented with Church whenever it is a 'vision free zone', and right to be fed up if Church is effectively www.millstone.org round our necks! It probably means we are right to pray fervently for a divine adrenaline injection into an institutional tombstone!

'Oh no, you can't criticise the Church,' some say. But have you ever thought that the very real sense of dissatisfaction many of us feel about Church may come from God? Who was it who said, 'People call out to God when the ground is shaking under their feet, only to discover it is God who is shaking it'?

We can't abandon Church in the sense that 'Church' comes with the package for Christian disciples, and at its best is absolutely indispensable. But that doesn't mean we simply accept all versions of Church, all expressions of Christian discipleship, all versions of Church 'acting' at being Church. It means that we must be committed to changing Church so that it becomes more truly Church, a community of people who resemble those Jesus urges us to become in the Sermon on the Mount. It's time for a change. Church needs to be transformed! We need to be transformed! And God wants to transform Church and us together.

Jesus' teaching makes it clear that we are to be kingdom people first and foremost, not Church people. We are to be about the business of the kingdom rather than Church. It is not that they are inevitably mutually exclusive, but it is that the kingdom outlook is to be our 'default' position. That's why, whenever we move into 'Church for Church sake' mode, we begin to experience a sense of incompleteness and dissatisfaction, a sense of 'we-weren't-called-to-be-like-this' ness.

> The church gets into trouble whenever it thinks it is in the church business rather than the kingdom business. In the church business people are concerned with church activities, religious behaviour and spiritual things. In the kingdom business, people are concerned with kingdom activities, all human behaviour and everything which God has made, visible and invisible. Church people think how to get people into the church, kingdom people think about how to get the church into the world. Church people worry that the world might change the church, kingdom people work to see the church change the world.
>
> Howard Snyder

70

In this teaching Jesus is not asking us about our religiosity. He is not asking about our commitment to an institution and its practices, even one which bears his name. Not

because such things are totally irrelevant, but because they are not the most important questions. We are to seek God's kingdom and God's righteousness, he says. Get that right and all else follows.

SECTION TWO
PRIORITIES FOR DISCIPLES
(Matthew 6:19-24)

In our house what gets done depends on who asks. I can ask my 18-year-old son to tidy his room until I'm blue in the face and he appears remarkably deaf to such requests. But when a certain young lady is coming round, without any asking, the room is sorted out – you can not only *see* the carpet, it is vacuumed as well!

Lying behind this teaching of Jesus is the question about who matters to you, who you are committed to, who is in charge of your life. Jesus is really saying 'Now, what are your priorities?' and he poses this question in relation to two issues that are as searching and relevant today as ever: wealth (or 'treasures') and masters.

Wealth

Do not store up for yourselves treasures on earth, where moth and rust consume and where thieves break in and steal; but store up for yourselves treasures in heaven, where neither moth nor rust consumes and where thieves do not break in and steal. For where your treasure is, there your heart will be also.

(Matthew 6:19-21)

71

In today's materialistic, consumer driven, money obsessed culture, there is no more telling way of ascertaining the priorities of a Christian disciple than talking about wealth.

Try this self-assessment text

- Do we hoard money?
- Do we find it hard to part with?
- When our investments increase do we get excited?
- When we lose money do we get depressed?
- Are our things more important to us than people?

Jesus makes it clear that problems are attached to wealth. Wealth causes people to think that they are self-sufficient. And when they think they are self-sufficient, they do not depend upon God. And when they don't depend upon God then it is harder for grace to rule their lives. And when grace doesn't rule their lives everything that Jesus identifies about discipleship becomes much harder to understand, accept and pursue.

When he was terminally ill, the TV entertainer Roy Castle received a letter from a show-biz millionaire. 'I can buy anything,' he wrote, 'but I know I've blown it.' Castle wrote back, 'No. There is always the possibility of change.'

Breaking the cycle – treasures in heaven

To those of us who *do* have treasures on earth – and some of us have a good deal of them – there is a way to begin to break the entrapping cycle. It is this. Deliberately and consciously begin to use your treasures on earth to make 'treasures in heaven'. Use it for the kingdom of God. Resource the work of the kingdom.

This means more than increasing regular giving to your local church. Despite the continuing numerical decline in most denominations in Britain I know of so many people who are called by God, 'sold out' for God, who have vision, through whom God's Spirit moves powerfully. I know young leaders through whom God wants to do so much, and really make a difference. All around us there are potentially exciting and effective ministries ready to go . . . and they are stymied by lack of support.

I believe this situation judges us. We protest loudly about the ineffectiveness, the lifelessness, the nominality, the irrelevance of much of what passes as Church. Then, when we recognise a project, a vision, a ministry that has the hallmark of God about it, and we *could* support it, and know we *should* support it – we don't.

The time for propping up leaking roofs, creaking causes and bleating ministries is over! We can't afford it. The time for sacrificially investing in kingdom projects, anointed ministries and visionary callings is here. We can't afford

Share together:
What are the Kingdom Projects
The Visionary Works
The Anointed Ministries known to you.

How do you respond to this application of Jesus' teaching on 'treasure'?

not to! We must take seriously Jesus' call to use treasures on earth to make treasures in heaven.

Consider very seriously then. How will you demonstrate to God and yourself, just where your priorities lie? You see, Jesus is more demanding than Dick Turpin. With him, it's your money *and* your life.

Masters

No one can serve two masters; for a slave will either hate the one and love the other, or be devoted to the one and despise the other. You cannot serve God and wealth.

(Matthew 6:24)

This section, like this teaching, is short and to the point. Jesus does not say you *shouldn't* serve two masters – he says you *can't*.

In the same way, you can't follow a road with a fork in it. You choose one way or another.

Jesus is asking, 'Who is your leader?' Not just for your ministry, or your life in church, but for the whole of your life. Who is actually, totally in control?

Some of us know that our lives, our key relationships are out of control. Drink, drugs of various sorts, lust, sex, language, the list is endless. Addiction is an awful thing; to some measure we all experience it, and in one sense carry with us that potential addiction all our days. But the root of all addiction is that things are not under control.

Jesus knows.

> And his word to us is not, 'Will you try harder?'
> Not, 'Will you have more willpower?'
> But, 'Will you let me by your master?
> Will you let me have control?'

Some of us need to hear that word above all others at this time.

Living martyrdom

In the early days of Christianity 'a life totally given to God' meant martyrdom. But over time, and certainly by the time the Celtic saints were around, they hit a problem. It was this. How do you become a martyr when no-one is actually trying to kill you? You can't goad someone to kill you or you lead him or her to commit murder, which is breaking God's law! The answer they arrived at, closely connected with monasticism, was a realisation that a person had to *live* as one whose life is irrevocably given to God. It was a living martyrdom, sometimes called 'white martyrdom'. This was their response to the call of Jesus to be one whose life is totally given to God.

Several of my friends trained for the Methodist ministry at Richmond College. In the 19th century it was a college from which dozens of people went to overseas mission fields on behalf of the Wesleyan Missionary Society. Apparently, in those days, at a weekly act of worship, the names of those who had died on the mission fields were read out and remembered. Then an invitation would be given. 'Who will go to replace them? Please stand and step forward.' And someone always stood and stepped forward.

Their names, their destination, the date they departed and the date they died were recorded on large wooden plaques which are now to be found in Methodist Church House, London. Time after time the date of departure and the date of death are only two or three years apart: 'John Barker, Africa, departed May 1834, died September 1836.'

But when did they die? In Africa in September 1836, or when they stood forward in the chapel at Richmond College?

What might 'a life totally given to God' mean today?

SECTION THREE
PROMISES ABOUT CARE AND FREEDOM
(Matthew 6:25-34)

Therefore I tell you, do not worry about your life, what you will eat or what you will drink, or about your body, what you will wear. Is not life more than food, and the body more than clothing? Look at the birds of the air; they neither sow nor reap nor gather into barns, and yet your heavenly Father feeds them. Are you not of more value than they? And can any of you by worrying add a single hour to your span of life? And why do you worry about clothing? Consider the lilies of the field, how they grow; they neither toil nor spin, yet I tell you, even Solomon in all his glory was not clothed like one of these. But if God so clothes the grass of the field, which is alive today and tomorrow is thrown into the oven, will he not much more clothe you – you of little faith? Therefore do not worry, saying, 'What will we eat?' or 'What will we drink?' or 'What will we wear?' For it is the Gentiles who strive for all these things; and indeed your heavenly Father knows that you need all these things. But strive first for the kingdom of God and his righteousness, and all these things will be given you as well . . .

Food. Drink. Clothes. Jesus identifies the very things that for many of us are central to the living of our lives. Never before in human history has life for so many consisted of what we eat and drink and what we wear. For many folk, these things determine and dominate who they feel they are.

> **To what extent do food, drink and clothes determine who we are?**

A TV programme recently interviewed several children and asked what they did when they were unhappy. 'I go shopping and buy something nice,' said one seven-year-old. Consumerism rules.

'Are you not worth much more?' says Jesus.

Those who make God their priority, discipleship of Jesus their loyalty, can expect the care of God which leads Jesus to say, 'So don't worry . . .' Birds and lilies are not nourished miraculously – in the sense of manna from heaven – but fed simply by the system to which they belong. Likewise, kingdom people are supplied with all they need through living in the kingdom. Seek that, says Jesus, and there is no need to worry, everything will sort itself out.
Seek God's kingdom and stop worrying! Easy, isn't it? Hardly. No wonder this is known as a 'hard saying' of Jesus, and one with which many of us wrestle. But it may be easier than we think . . .

Jesus suggests that if we have only one account, marked 'all for God in Jesus Christ' then we've got it all where it ought to be. If there are things in our lives that won't fit into that account, then we don't need them anyway! There is only one absolute demand upon our lives, and that's the demand of God in Christ Jesus. Every other demand is relative to that. Wow!

This mind-blowing teaching is actually one of the kindest things Jesus ever said, because when you've got to that point, you are really free. There is nothing anybody can do to you that ultimately matters. What will they take if you don't have anything? How does someone threaten to take away your life if you've given it away already? While you have things in other accounts, you'll never be free. But when it is all truly given to him, you're free. When you belong to Jesus Christ, you are free!

> Are you free?
> Have you anything to lose?
> If so, give it to him quick.
> Seek first the kingdom of God,
> And all these things will be added to you.
> May God help us to do that.

LIVING IN THE KINGDOM AND LIVING OUT THE GOSPEL

(Matthew 7)

> Read Matthew 7. If you are in a group, allocate the several sections to different readers but read the *whole* chapter at this point. Assuming that all the material relating to chapter 7 is not studied in one meeting, you may want to read the chapter at the start of each meeting dealing with this material.

The Sermon on the Mount and the Great Commission

At the end of Matthew's gospel is a passage commonly known as the 'Great Commission'. The risen Jesus instructs his disciples to 'Go into all the world and make disciples, baptising them . . . and teaching them to obey everything that I have commanded you.' Teaching 'everything that I have commanded you' most certainly includes teaching the Sermon on the Mount. Therefore, what is studied here is basic information for all would-be Christian disciples. Already we have found that Jesus' teaching involves not just believing, but also involves being and doing and living and dying. It is, to use a 'posh' term, about 'orthopraxis', not just 'orthodoxy'. It's not simply about 'doctrines' but about living out a relationship. The Sermon on the Mount relates how a Parent God wants his children to live.

The varied material in chapter 7 focuses on orthopraxis – about living in the kingdom and living out the gospel. Jesus makes it clear that for his disciples the kingdom of God is not something you simply learn about, but a reign of God in which you live. It is about doing the gospel.

> **Share with one another:**
>
> **What is the most important spiritual insight you have grasped from the Sermon on the Mount so far?**
>
> **What difference has it made in your life?**

The Sermon on the Mount is about *the difference* that seeking to be disciples of Jesus makes in thought, word and deed.

> *Truly this is a new people, and there is something divine in them.*
>
> Aristedes to Emperor Hadrian about 2nd century Christians

A kingdom of righteousness

Rumbling along under the text of the Sermon on the Mount is the question 'What is the kingdom of God about?' To which the answer is given with the regularity of a heartbeat: it is a kingdom of righteousness. The term 'righteousness' is used repeatedly in the Sermon on the Mount, and used in a number of ways.

In some instances 'righteousness' means 'being right', that is 'being right with God'. And because God alone is 'right', God alone has the ability to 'put us right' and does this through the atoning death of Jesus Christ, the Son of God.

In some instances 'righteousness' means 'doing right', that is performing righteousness – quite literally, doing the right thing.

In some instances 'righteousness' means 'being in a right relationship with others' or 'putting in a right relationship with others'.

> *God is Right,*
> *Does Right,*
> *and Puts in the Right.*

Each of these usages of righteousness are found in the Sermon on the Mount and each derives from God who, as Donald English often used to remind his hearers, Is Right, Does Right, and Puts in the Right. This is the nature of God who reigns in this kingdom.

Three main sections

As with the previous chapter, Jesus' teaching can be helpfully split into three sections.

- Section one (7:1-6) revisits the issue of our relationships with *others*
- Section two (7:7-12) revisits the issue of our relationship with *God*
- Section three (7:13-29) revisits the issue of our *discipleship of Jesus.*

SECTION ONE
'JUDGE LIKE THIS . . .'
the disciple's relationship with others
(Matthew 7:1–5)

Do not judge, so that you may not be judged. For with the judgement you make you will be judged, and the measure you give will be the measure you get. Why do you see the speck in your neighbour's eye, but do not notice the log in your own eye? Or how can you say to your neighbour, 'Let me take the speck out of your eye,' while the log is in your own eye? You hypocrite, first take the log out of your own eye, and then you will see clearly to take the speck out of your neighbour's eye.

Those who say Jesus had no sense of humour have obviously never read this passage. Surely it is a joke from a carpenter turned preacher, told with a smile? Jesus knows the size of a log or 'mote' and knows it could take two men to lift it. So he presents us with this almost comic cartoon image of a person, five foot two in their sandals, with a 12-foot log stuck in their eye. Jesus would also know how excruciating it is when you get the smallest speck of sawdust in your eye, and how big that smallest speck feels to be.

A Scotsman staying in a hotel came down to breakfast and sat next to a man at a table. 'This is a strange hotel,' he said. 'Why is that?' replied the man. 'Well, about half-past three this morning there was hammering on my walls and shouting. It was really quite frightening.' 'Didn't you go and investigate?' said the man, 'or contact the Reception?' 'No, I didn't. I decided just to mind my own business and carried on playing my bagpipes.'

In this passage Jesus is talking about the folk who are oblivious of their own faults, but try to sort out everyone else's. This is a fault common to many of us. We use two sets of scales, one to weigh the faults of others, another to weigh our own faults. In 'them' it is a sin, in 'us' merely a 'minor flaw'; in 'them' it's lust, in 'us' it's 'just natural'! I am told that some women (and presumably men) choose which shop windows they will look in to catch their reflection. Apparently some windows make you appear more 'right' than others.

Jesus is saying, 'Help your brother and sister, but make sure you are sorted out yourself first.'

A woman brought her son to Mahatma Gandhi and asked him to tell her son to stop eating sugar. 'Come back next week,' he said. The woman was a bit disappointed, but turned up the following week with her son. Gandhi sat the boy on his knee and said gently, 'Now do as your mother asks, don't eat sugar, it's bad for you.' He hugged the lad and sent him on his way. The woman said, 'Thank you, Bapu, but why couldn't you do that last week?' Gandhi replied with a smile, 'Because last week, I too was eating sugar.'

Judgement leading to ministry

Once a person is sorted out, once they have judged themselves rightly, they are in a position to help. You only remove foreign bodies from someone's eye when you've had a good scrub up, and when you can see to do it. Consequently there is as much about *ministry* in this passage as judgement.

The 'logless' disciple is now in a position to remove the splinter from the eye of her sister. Pain is relieved. After some eye watering, she can see again. It is – quite literally – 'body' ministry! But removing splinters from someone's eye is a delicate operation. Despite the excruciating pain, the patient will only let someone they trust near them.

Do you see? All these images are of brothers and sisters 'fine tuned' and 'steady handed' to the needs of each other.

Now contrast this sensitive, trusting, discerning business with the finger-pointing, gossip-ridden, spiteful, party cliquishness, and the cynical, sharp, judgemental attitudes that sadly sometimes characterise our life together in Christ. Doves over Communion cups and piranhas over tea cups!

Any local church of any size probably has some of them:

Posturing Paul	Materialistic Marion
Gossiping Glad	Religious Reginald
Judgemental Julian	Critical Carol

Some of you may have watched on TV – to keep your children company, of course! – *Big Brother*. The plot is simple. Put 10 volunteers, hand-picked from the thousands that

In the Christian Big Brother House called the local church, what would <u>you</u> get thrown out for?

offered, into a house for 10 weeks, and watch them. Each week the 'inmates' nominate two of their number for eviction, and the general public selects which one of the two is 'out on their ear' through a telephone vote. And so on until there is only one left in the house – the winner. In the Christian Big Brother House called the local church, what would *you* get thrown out for?

Does it make any difference to you whether this teaching relates to everyone or only to the family of Christ?

Experts are divided about who is included in this teaching on judgement (and much else of the teaching in the Sermon). Is Jesus talking about our relationships with everyone, or only those in the Church, the family of Christ? Matthew gives little guidance as he describes the listeners to this sermon as both 'disciples' and 'the crowd'.

The comic cartoon approach of Jesus contains a strong punch-line. He reminds us that the law God operates is the law of reciprocity. How we judge others determines how God deals with

How is your discipleship in this area?

us. This is a serious business. How you get on with your brothers and sisters determines how you get on with God.

SECTION TWO
'ASK . . . SEEK . . . KNOCK . . .'
the disciple's relationship with God
(Matthew 7:7–11)

Ask, and it will be given to you; search, and you will find; knock, and the door will be opened for you. For everyone who asks receives, and everyone who searches finds, and for everyone who knocks, the door will be opened. Is there anyone among you who, if your child asks for bread, will give a stone? Or if the child asks for a fish, will give a snake? If you then, who are evil, know how to give good gifts to your children, how much more will your Father in heaven give good things to those who ask him!

Asking, seeking and knocking are all images of prayer in the Old Testament, and the Jews on the mountainside listening to Jesus would know that.

Repeated asking

Did you notice how often the word 'ask' occurs in this passage?

Proud people in particular find it very hard to ask for things. Self-sufficiency is deadly for disciples. So perhaps some of us just need to hear a word that goes like this: 'You do not receive more, because you do not ask enough.'

'You do not receive more, because you do not ask enough.' Is that you?

Active seeking

Then there is seeking, which is an active participation in the process of asking.

'Can I have a sandwich for lunch?' I said to Helen, my wife. 'Yes, love,' she replied. Twenty minutes later I realised it hadn't arrived and as she walked by I asked again, 'Please, can I have a sandwich?' 'Go and find it!' she said. There it was, all ready, in the kitchen. It was a simple move, really, from the armchair to the kitchen, but I would have gone hungry if I hadn't made it!

There is asking, then the follow-up to asking. It is doubtful that the lost sheep (in Luke 15) would have been found without the shepherd going out to seek it. It is unlikely that the lost coin (also in Luke 15) would have turned up, had the woman not searched the house. Seeking is our part of the process.

What are we doing in our lives that resembles active 'seeking', and especially seeking for those things we know we need in order to be kingdom people?

What are we doing in our lives that resembles active 'seeking'?

Keep on knocking

Knocking suggests persistency. Keep on asking and seeking and bringing those things before God.

Some commentators have discerned a progression in this text. Imagine a visitor to a region, say Yorkshire. They **ask** the destination (say Harrogate), **seek** the location (which house and street in Harrogate), and **knock** for entry; when the location is discovered, each facet becomes more precise. For some this will appear a bit convoluted, but the biblical emphasis is clear: when you pray you will be heard. The answer may be 'no' but you will still be heard.

Do you accept 'no' as an answer to your requests to God? Or do you regard 'no' as a prayer that 'didn't work' or wasn't answered?

That wonderfully common word 'will'

There is only one other word as common as 'ask' in this section, and that is the word 'will'. Jesus affirms that when you ask you *will* be heard; when you seek you *will* find, and when you knock the way *will* open up. God can be trusted to meet our requests appropriately.

The best 'askers', 'seekers' and 'knockers' in my life are my children. Not strangers who knock on the door and want to sell dusters, but family. Asking, seeking and knocking is not simply a rough guide to doctrine, but the description of a family. It suggests a live relationship, an interactive relationship, a wrestling relationship, an intimate relationship, between God and the children of God.

> Jesus reminds us that prayer is a little like children coming to their parents. Our children come to us with the craziest requests at times. Often we are grieved by the meanness and selfishness of their requests, but we would be all the more grieved if they never came to us even with their meanness and selfishness. We are simply glad that they do come – mixed motives and all.
>
> Alan Storkey

Children ask for all sorts of things, but sometimes don't know what's best for them. Like children, we ask God for all sorts of things and often we don't know what's best for us. But God does know what's best for us. God sees through our words, and gives not always what we say we want, but what the Father knows we need. For disciples, that is enough.

The 'how much more' God . . .

If you then, who are evil, know how to give good gifts to your children, how much more will your Father in heaven give good things to those who ask him!

(Matthew 7:11)

I find that this wonderful image of a parent God – a 'how much more' God – is best grasped by stories.

Losing Sam

When my children were young we spent several summer holidays 'camping' in France; camping for softies, where the tent and beds are all ready for you. According to the Michelin map the campsite looked no distance at all, but it took hours longer than expected to get there and we arrived well after 11 at night. The sleepy courier, who had been expecting us since 7pm, met us and showed us to our plot. The campsite was quiet and dark and we tried to make as little noise as possible as we got organised. Helen took our three boys to the washrooms to get ready for bed while I unloaded what we needed and put the kettle on.

Then followed one of those occasions when you go cold in a split second. It was around midnight and we were sipping tea. I looked in the boys' compartment and said, 'Where's Sam?' 'He's in bed, isn't he? He was the first to get ready for bed. I sent him over ages ago.' Panic was rising in our voices. It was then that we realised that within half an hour of arriving on a strange, sleeping, foreign campsite we had 'misplaced' our four-year-old son.

Every fibre of my body wanted to leap outside the tent and yell 'Sam' at the top of my voice. Instead, we did the 'British' thing, creeping around the tents hissing his name as loud as we dare. It was the longest few minutes of my life. He was found on a swing next to one of three swimming pools on the site – and (at that time) he couldn't swim.

I cannot relate the sense of relief when we found him. Suddenly it didn't matter that his first play school report suggested he was not likely to become a brain surgeon. It was of no consequence that his bedroom usually resembled a stock-take in a charity shop. All that mattered was that he was lost and had been found.

And Jesus says, 'How much more . . ?'

Therapy

A therapist met a new woman patient. 'Tell me,' he said, 'which of your children do you love the most?' The woman replied instantly, 'I love all my children equally.' 'No human being is able to love three or four humans equally,' commented the therapist. 'If I am to be of any help to you, you've got to be honest, now tell me the truth.' The woman became tearful. 'All right, all right,' she said. 'When one of my children is ill, I love that one the most. When one of my children is sad, I love that one the most. When one of my children is upset, I love that one the most. When one of my children is bad, I love that one the most. Because you see, I'm their mother.'

And Jesus says, 'How much more . . ?'

Steve's testimony

Steve is a missionary in South America. He arrived at an international conference in Spring 2000, just a few days after burying his 20-year-old daughter.

He was invited to give a word of testimony. He stood on the stage with two members of the tribe among whom he worked. He told how his father had also been a missionary in South America, 40 years earlier, working among the same tribe with which Steve now worked. Steve's dad had been killed when Steve was a small boy, by a member of the tribe, and Steve emotionally recounted how his father's death had affected him. Then he introduced one of the men with him and it became clear that this was the man who had killed his father. The man had become a Christian and as a consequence of that had decided to take the place of the man of God he had killed. Steve described his love for the man, and the love of his children for the man, who was known by Steve's children as 'Granddad'.

I confess I don't understand forgiveness like that. But glorious though it is, it is only a shadow of God's forgiveness.

And Jesus says, 'How much more . . ?'

Mother and child

A mother is walking round the lounge with her new-born baby. She hugs it to her and sings a tuneless song. She looks at the baby and smiles, and the baby smiles back.

What has this baby done to be so accepted, so loved? Well, it has been sick all over her twice so far that morning. It has brought enormous disruption to the family. The family income has reduced considerably at the same time as the expenses have increased. She has lost her 'shape' and her hormones are all over the place. And she looks at her baby, smiles, and kisses it.

And Jesus says, 'How much more . . ?' How much more will the Father give?

With which of these stories do you most identify? Have you any other 'how much more' stories you want to share? What is God saying to you?

The Golden Rule

In everything do to others as you would have them do to you; for this is the law and the prophets.

(Matthew 7:12)

This statement is sometimes known as the Golden Rule, and it brings to an end a block of teaching which began in Matthew 5 and concerned Jesus' teaching in relation to the Ten Commandments.

The Ten Commandments can be effectively split into two parts. The first four commandments are 'vertical', that is, they relate to God (eg. 'You shall have no other gods but me'). The last six commandments are 'horizontal', that is, they concern our dealings with other people (eg. Do not steal or murder).

In the first 12 verses of Matthew 7, Jesus deals with those two issues in reverse order. The first six verses (about judging) concern our dealings with others and the latter six (about asking, seeking and knocking) relate to God.

This verse, then, is Jesus' summary of his teaching on the law: 'In everything do to others as you would have them do to you.'

How do you want to be treated by God? With grace and mercy, or with justice? I'll take grace and mercy every time! I know what justice requires, but I pray for mercy, and the Sermon on the Mount gives me confidence to pray for mercy.

As far as you are concerned in your dealings with others – justice or mercy?
As far as you hope in God's dealings with you – justice or mercy?

SECTION THREE
STORIES OF DECISION AND CHOICE
the disciple's relationship with Jesus Christ
(Matthew 7:13–29)

Decisions, decisions

The remainder of the Sermon on the Mount concerns stories of decisions and choices. This narrow gate or that wide one? Good fruit from a good tree or bad fruit from a bad tree? Saying 'Jesus is Lord' and meaning it, or just saying it? Laying foundations on rock or on sand? The decision, the choice, says Jesus, is yours. But these decisions and choices define the extent and true nature of Christian discipleship.

Two gates – the route to life

Enter through the narrow gate; for the gate is wide and the road is easy that leads to destruction, and there are many who take it. For the gate is narrow and the road is hard that leads to life, and there are few who find it.

(Matthew 7:13-14)

The first section of teaching about decision and choice concerns images of gates and travel and makes it clear that discipleship of Jesus demands effort. It is a 'hard road' to travel. It's like a long uphill walk. This is, after all, a sermon on a *mount* and those who were present to hear Jesus had made an effort to be there. No wonder they were breathless!

> *Here's my tip for running the marathon, start slowly and taper off.*
> Steve Rider,
> Sports Presenter on BBC TV

When so much in life today is about quick fixes we do well to remember that Christian discipleship is long-haul stuff. It is more like a marathon than a sprint.

92

Increasingly we need to see the notion of Christian conversion as long-term, long-haul discipleship of Jesus Christ. It has always been so.

Is that a description of our Christian discipleship?

Think for a moment, when was Simon Peter converted?

- When Jesus called him from the lakeside?
- When Jesus called him Peter and gave him the keys of the kingdom?
- At the Transfiguration of Jesus?
- In the darkness of the courtyard as he hated himself for denying Jesus?
- As he ran away from the empty tomb?
- At the seashore when he said three times, 'Yes, Lord, you know I love you'?
- On the day of Pentecost when he was filled with the Holy Spirit?
- At the house of Cornelius when he realised God shows no favourites?
- On his own cross, upside down, outside Rome, moments before his death?

Yes, yes, yes, yes, yes! All of these. Discipleship is a lifelong thing. It is a life of constantly choosing the route to life, of consciously opting for the narrow gate time after time.

Discipleship is always in the 'renewing present' tense of our lives, and is a choice we make at each change of life.

Marriage	and, for some, divorce
When children arrive	and when they leave
When children don't arrive	ever
In long-term illness	and mid-life crisis
At retirement	and bereavement

At each point we are invited to reaffirm our discipleship. We choose the route to life, we choose Jesus. It may be that some of us need to choose Jesus in a time of life change. Is that you?

> **Think quietly:**
> **Have I given my life to Christ, then taken it back again?**
> **Have I moved through some 'change of life' but not reaffirmed my discipleship of Jesus through it?**
> **If so, is it time to do that now?**

I remember Baz, a part-time student at Cliff College, sitting on a chair in the college Conference Centre, suddenly beginning to cry. Why? Because, he told me later, he suddenly became acutely aware that exactly 20 years before he had first given his life to Christ, in exactly the same place. He had become overwhelmed by memories, and by an awareness of God's leading over two decades of ups and downs. He had also become overwhelmingly aware of God's leading and faithfulness through it all. That day, Baz continued being converted. He hadn't left the narrow way but he chose it again and reaffirmed his discipleship of Jesus.

False teachers and right fruit

Beware of false prophets, who come to you in sheep's clothing but inwardly are ravenous wolves. You will know them by their fruits. Are grapes gathered from thorns, or figs from thistles? In the same way, every good tree bears good fruit, but the bad tree bears bad fruit. A good tree cannot bear bad fruit, nor can a bad tree bear good fruit. Every tree that does not bear good fruit is cut down and thrown into the fire. Thus you will know them by their fruits.

(Matthew 7:15-20)

I love watching the *Antiques Roadshow* on TV. Perversely, I find two scenarios almost as thrilling as each other. The first is when you hold your breath as the expert declares something that most folk wouldn't look twice at is a rare and genuine piece worth many thousands of pounds. The second is when the expert pauses, then says, 'Well, *if* this were genuine . . !'

In his next story of decision and choice Jesus contrasts things false and true and uses the image of a tree bearing good or bad fruit.

Disciples are to beware false teachers who will be known ultimately by their fruits: what is true inside will show itself outside. False teachers may have all the right words and apparently the right works, they may declare the right creed and

> Are 'fruits' a better guarantee of true discipleship than 'gifts'? What do you think?

apparently the right deeds, they may make the right professions and apparently do the right expressions of faith. But it will be a lie – by their fruits, what is produced and grown over time – will you know truth from what is false.

Jesus seems to be suggesting that in God's kingdom gifts are less of a guarantee of discipleship than fruit, because fruit can't be faked.

> *What a pity that so hard on the heels of Christ come the Christians!*
>
> Annie Dillard

Self-deception

Not everyone who says to me, 'Lord, Lord', will enter the kingdom of heaven, but only the one who does the will of my Father in heaven. On that day many will say to me, 'Lord, Lord, did we not prophesy in your name, and cast out demons in your name, and do many deeds of power in your name?' Then I will declare to them, 'I never knew you; go away from me, you evildoers.'

(Matthew 7:21-23)

I want to point out three things about this apparently hard teaching of Jesus, the third teaching of decision and choice.

Three B's – not one!

First, Jesus seems to differentiate between what a person *says* and what they *believe*. Clearly in his mind there is more to belief than simply saying you believe. Consequently it is possible to assert belief, or faith, and not truly possess it. Some say, 'Lord, Lord', but there isn't a calorie of value in the whole thing!

This is a salutary word to us today. In relatively recent times to 'believe' something *has* largely been understood as what is affirmed, what is *stated*. But an older, better tradition of Christian discipleship would regard this as a weak and diluted notion of what true belief was.

> **Believing**
> **Belonging**
> **Behaviour**
> The marks of a lasting, mature discipleship?

In the early centuries, for example, it was clear that discipleship consisted of three 'B's', not one. Discipleship was Belief, Belonging, and Behaviour. You believed in Jesus, belonged to him – and therefore to his people – and made clear your discipleship of him in your behaviour and lifestyle. Take any 'B' out of the reckoning and discipleship became incomplete. *Saying* 'Lord, Lord' was not enough. At its best Christian discipleship has always been more than what is said.

Am I guilty of just 'saying' it?

Consequently discipleship is more than giving verbal assent to certain doctrines, mentally ticking off stanzas of a creed. A biographer of the great American evangelist Dwight L. Moody wrote, 'In the back of that shoe store in Boston, Moody gave himself and his life to Christ.' Discipleship is about giving yourself and your life. David Watson was hinting at the same thing when he commented, 'We call many to belief, but few to obedience.' There is much more to all this than saying, 'Lord, Lord', but to say it and mean it and live it out is a wonderful thing.

> *The people who least live the creeds are not seldom the people who shout loudest about them. The paralysis which affects the arms does not, in these cases, interfere with the tongue . . . That which a person believes, they live by. All the rest is religious froth.*
>
> Unknown

An other-worldly kingdom, a private, inward looking spirit, a God-in-my-pocket, a spiritualised, neutered Bible, an escapist church, all these make Christian 'conversion' possible without any drastic change in lifestyle and value systems. But true discipleship is about being converted every day. Jesus says to his disciples, in effect, 'Are you going to be my shape, or am I going to be yours?'

Service, not 'self'

Secondly, as in so many cases in the Sermon on the Mount Jesus places crucial importance on the *motives* of a person. Some of those who say, 'Lord, Lord' have the wrong motives. They see themselves as 'employees' not children of the Father. Consequently all they do 'in his name' is about giving *service*, whereas Jesus seems more interested in people giving *themselves*. Self, not service, is the fundamental requirement of discipleship.

> In my discipleship of Christ am I giving service, but not giving 'myself'?

Who's using who?

Thirdly, some of those who say, 'Lord, Lord' are using Jesus as means to an end. Notice how often in the text 'we' appears. It is 'we' prophesied, 'we' cast out demons, 'we' did mighty works. The name of Jesus has become a mantra. These people are using him, rather than he using them, and in a false, negative and unhealthy way.

> In your Christian discipleship who is using who? In what ways? And is it healthy?

In themselves, believers have no life, or strength, or spiritual power. All that they have of vital religion comes from Christ. They are what they are, and feel what they feel, and do what they do, because they draw out of Jesus a continual supply of grace, help and ability. Joined to the Lord by faith, and united in mysterious union with him by the Spirit, they stand, and walk, and continue, and run the Christian race.

J. C. Ryle

Hearers and doers

Everyone then who hears these words of mine and acts on them will be like a wise man who built his house on rock. The rain fell, the floods came, and the winds blew and beat on that house, but it did not fall, because it had been founded on rock. And everyone who hears these words of mine and does not act on them will be like a foolish man who built his house on sand. The rain fell, and the floods came, and the winds blew and beat against that house, and it fell – and great was its fall!

(Matthew 7:24-27)

Jesus' final story of decision and choice is a story of two men. How alike they were in so many ways. Both heard Jesus' words. Both probably sang the same hymns and songs. Both may have attended the same synagogue. Both read the same scriptures. Both experienced the same storm, wind and rain. Both were builders.

The difference was that one was wise and the other wasn't. Why? Because one acted on Jesus' words and the other didn't.

Those who are right with Jesus are those who are right with his teaching. They hear it and act on it. There will still be storms in the lives of the wise and the foolish alike, the difference is that the wise will stand.

> *Those who are right with Jesus are those who are right with his teaching.*

Who is your foundation? Jesus states that a relationship with God is the only true foundation on which to build our lives. Jesus' teaching enables us to enter that relationship with God, to live in the kingdom – all else is shifting sand.

A student of A. N. Whitehead, the English Professor of Philosophy at Harvard University, once came to talk to him. 'Professor, I think your understanding of the universe is all wrong.' 'Really, how do you understand it?' 'I think the universe is a turtle.' 'Hmm,' said Whitehead, 'and what is under that turtle?' 'Another turtle.' 'I see,' said Whitehead, 'and what is . . .' Getting the idea of the line of questions the student broke in. 'Look, Professor,' he said, 'it's turtles all the way down!' Now what is it with us that is 'all the way down'?

> **What is it with us that is 'all the way down'?**

Have you noticed that in each of these teachings about decisions and choices first impressions are contrasted with lasting fruit? There is no short cut to the kind of discipleship that we are talking about here.

Learning something and living it are two different things. The Sermon on the Mount makes it plain that discipleship of Jesus Christ isn't truly learned, until it's lived.

I want to be like . . . the imitation of Christ

When Jesus had come down from the mountain, great crowds followed him . . .

(Matthew 8:1)

I remember David Wilkinson saying, 'When I was young I wanted to be like Superman. When I got older I wanted to be like Mel Gibson. I don't wish that anymore . . . but my wife still does! But in the end there is only one person that I want to be like . . .' And he went on to talk about Jesus.

Jesus Christ:

The One who went into the wilderness for 40 days, tempted by the devil in so many ways, but who resisted evil.

The One who taught with authority, who was filled with love, and radiated the power of God.

The One who brought healing and wholeness to those he met.

The One who accepted those who were rejected and outcast by society.

The One who loved the sinner and rejected the sin.

The One who valued people.

The One whose supreme love enabled him to give his life for others.

The One who was arrested, and in the trauma of his arrest on false charges, healed the ear of his enemy.

The One who was rejected and betrayed by his friends but kept on loving them.

The One who was mocked and jeered, beaten and whipped, but did not lash out with hand or words.

The One who was put on a cross with nails through his hands and feet . . . and went on loving.

The One who, in this terrible situation, speaks kindly to a petrified thief saying, 'Today you will be with me in paradise.'

The One, who in the midst of all of this, said, 'Father, forgive them, they don't know what they are doing.'

Disciples are those who want to be like that, who are possessed with a desire to be like Jesus.

> *. . . the Sermon on the Mount . . . I have fallen under its spell, or rather under the spell of him who preached it.*
>
> John Stott

To have such a desire burning in your heart is to be in a position to encounter the Sermon on the Mount – Jesus' manual of discipleship.

When Jesus came down the mountain he lived out what he taught.

When Jesus came down the mountain great crowds followed him.

Let's resolve to go and do the same, in the power of the Spirit of God.

REFERENCES AND SOURCES USED

I urge readers to get these and use them.

Martyn Atkins, 'The Great Commission' in *Beyond the Fringes* (Methodist Church Home Mission, 1996).

Donald English, *An Evangelical Theology of Preaching* (Abingdon, 1996).

Richard Foster, *Prayer – finding the heart's true home* (Hodder & Stoughton, 1993).

Richard Foster, *Streams of Living Water* (HarperCollins, 1999).

Rob Frost, *Sharing Jesus in the new millennium* (Scripture Union, 2000).

Stanley Hauerwas and William Willimon, *Resident Aliens* (Abingdon, 1989).

Tony Hancock script by Simpson, Galton & Stott, © Castle Communications PLC, 1997.

James Jones, *Following Jesus* (Bible Reading Fellowship, 1993).

Gerard Kelly, *Get a Grip on the Future with losing your hold on the past* (Monarch, 1999).

R. T. Kendall, *Just Grace* (SPCK, 2000).

'King of the Hill': Spring Harvest Study Guide 2001 (Spring Harvest, 2001).

C. S. Lewis, *Christian Behaviour* (Bles: Centenary Press, 1943).

Martyn Lloyd-Jones, *Studies in the Sermon on the Mount* (2 volumes) (IVP, 1960).

Jeff Lucas, *Lucas on Life* (Paternoster, 2001).

Rebecca Manley Pippert, *Out of the Saltshaker* (IVP, revised edition 1998).

Charles Price, *Matthew* (Christian Focus, 1998).

Mike Regele (with Mark Schulz), *Death of the Church* (Zondervan, 1996).

Clyde Reid, *Groups Alive – Church Alive* (Harper & Row, 1969).

Michael Riddell, *Threshold of the Future* (SPCK, 1998).

J. C. Ryle, *Holiness: Its Nature, Hindrances, Difficulties, and Roots* (Charles Nolan Publishing, 2001).

J. C. Ryle, *Matthew* (Crossway books, 1993).

Howard Snyder, *Liberating the Church* (IVP, 1983).

Alan Storkey, *Jesus* (Christian Studies Press, 2000).

John Stott, *The Message of the Sermon on the Mount* (IVP, 1978).

The Methodist Worship Book, (Methodist Publishing House, 1999).

Rob Warner, *Praying with Jesus* (Hodder & Stoughton, 1999).

David Watson, *Discipleship* (Hodder & Stoughton, 1981).

Rob Warner, *The Sermon on the Mount* (Kingsway, 1998).

Philip Yancey, *The Jesus I never knew* (Marshall Pickering, 1995).